MW01615314

Process Based Management: A Foundation for Business Excellence

Process Based Management:

A Foundation for Business Excellence

Dennis C. Daly
Metropolitan State University

Patrick L. Dowdle
Process Advantage, Inc.

Robert T. McCarty
United States Coast Guard

Jerry W. Stevens
Stevens Group, Inc.

© Copyright 2004, CAM-I
All Rights Reserved.

No part of this book may be reproduced, stored in
a retrieval system, or transmitted by any means,
electronic, mechanical, photocopying, recording,
or otherwise, without written permission
from CAM-I.

119 NE Wilshire Blvd., Suite E
Burleson, TX 76028

ISBN: 1-59453-461-6

Bookman LLC
Publishing & Marketing
**Providing Quality, Professional
Author Services**

www.BookmanMarketing.com

ACKNOWLEDGEMENTS

Developed at CAM-I through the Collaborative efforts of:

Dan Callot- IBM
Dean Creed- Santee Cooper
Dennis Daly- Metropolitan State University
Pat Dowdle-Process Advantage
Poul Tonny Kjaer- StatOil
Mark McKee: Honeywell
Michael McCain- United States Air Force
Robert McCarty- United States Coast Guard
Jerry Stevens- Stevens Group, Inc
Phil Yeich- SAS
Peter von Zimmermann- SAP
Faheem Zuberi- Fleet Boston/Bank of America

PREFACE

This book is the second in a series of three books on CAM-I's Process Based Management Research that began in 1994. The first book **"The Road to Excellence: Becoming a Process-Based Company"** published in 1997, was to inform and educate organizations about Process Based Management. It is a real world consolidation of process based management experiences and provides an educational vehicle for management and workers to foster a better understanding of process based management. The success and survival of an organization depend on how well the organization manages its processes.

This second book in the series, **Process Based Management: A Foundation for Business Excellence**, published in 2004, is targeted at organizations and individuals who are on the road to Process Based Management. We assume that the reader has some level of understanding, and has experienced some of the challenges on this journey. To establish the starting point, we reiterate what we mean by Process Based Management and its benefits.

This book arose from the need to validate the process based management framework developed in the original research. There was a concern that the model may have value only to the particular organizations involved in the original research. To address that concern, an assessment framework model and questionnaire were developed to conduct the validation effort. The framework was applied to several in-depth case studies, focusing on a significantly different set of organizations than those involved in the original research.

During the course of this research it became necessary to extend the definition of Process Based Management and the case for adopting this approach as a fundamental part of an organizations management philosophy. This research process led to the development of a Discipline Model, Process Based Management Assessment Framework, and a Process Continuum Model as essential building blocks. This book is the result of this phase of the research.

As we complete this work in 2004, Business Process Management (BPM) has begun to get traction in the information technology and business press. We have not addressed the linkage of IT systems into the evolving BPM model. However, for BPM to be successful, Process Based Management will need to be in place in organizations. This linkage will be addressed in the next book.

The third volume, **Implementing Process Based Management**, will capture the essential "how" issue that is fundamental to the adoption of Process Based Management. This volume will be built on our previous research and based on extensive Process Based Management best practices research (currently underway). This volume will depict the in-depth study of the implementation process adopted by these organizations and an implementation road map.

EXECUTIVE SUMMARY

In today's business environment, organizations are experiencing pain they can no longer ignore. It is imperative that organizations challenge existing practices and evolve in ways that address these pressures. Organizations need a roadmap on how to address these issues in a coordinated and integrated approach. They need insight into an evolving management approach that focuses on the processes in an organization in a holistic manner to improve both customer service and the efficiency and effectiveness of the organization. We call that approach Process Based Management.

This book expands on the nature and benefits of Process Based Management and presents some fundamental models that organizations can use to identify gaps in their process-based efforts. The models provide characteristics and attributes that would be seen as an organization progresses along the road to becoming a process-based organization.

Most organizations have realized the importance of managing processes, and have deployed various initiatives to improve their processes. What was apparent from our research and case studies was that many organizations have no way to assess how they are doing as they progress along the journey to becoming process-based. The research indicated the need for a:

- Way to communicate the strategic view of Process Based Management
- Means to evaluate the management approach of an organization
- Method to determine the level of maturity of Process Based Management in an organization

To address these needs, the "Process Based Management Loop" was developed. This loop is the foundation for assessing an organization's process-based efforts and provides a conceptual structure showing how the different models interact.

The first model in the Loop is the **Discipline Model**. The Discipline model is a conceptual framework that an organization would use to gain an understanding of how their tools, methods, and initiatives support the business model and their overall management philosophy. This linkage to a management philosophy will enable an organization to select and implement the appropriate methods and tools to support their specific business direction and strategy.

The second model is the **Process Based Management Assessment** Model, which provides an overall assessment of an organization's progress in implementing Process Based

Management. Using the categories depicted in the assessment framework, an organization would work through the assessment process to determine those areas it does well (their strengths) and identify the categories where additional efforts are needed (their gaps). The overall results from the assessment are then evaluated to determine the organization's maturity level in implementing Process Based Management.

The maturity levels lead us to the final model in the loop, the Process Continuum Model, which has been developed to identify and capture the characteristics an organization should have, or needs to acquire, during the transformation to Process Based Management. The Process Continuum Model can also assist an organization in progressing to the next level of maturity by identifying the characteristics of the next level, which aids in the development of specific action plans to improve their overall Process Based Management maturity.

If your organization is on the journey to becoming process-based, this book will provide insight and approaches to help your organization be more successful.

FOREWORD

CAM-I has been at the leading edge of developments in the field of cost management for over 20 years. We have been at the forefront of knowledge in Activity-based Costing and Activity-based Management for as long as the concepts have existed, and have been involved in development of ABCM methodology for almost as long. Our work has extended the "cost management" body of knowledge into related fields such as capacity measurement, activity-based planning & budgeting, target costing, and process based management.

All of these efforts and developments have focused on business information and approaches that assessed the past or present. The work in process management has taken a different path. When the interest group to explore process management was formed in 1993, a group of companies came together that had been heavily engaged in business process reengineering. This approach had reduced costs, but had negatively impacted customer and employee satisfaction. There had to be a better way. What they realized was that a process approach was the key for lasting benefits. That process approach was identified in the 1997 book, "The Road to Excellence: Becoming a Process-Based Company."

I would be remiss to not recognize the many contributions to this follow-on book. Many people and organizations helped shape the thinking as the group explored the various aspects of Process Based Management.

The case study organizations provided our project team with the opportunity to test both the assessment framework and the overall process. Significant knowledge and insight was gained from these case studies and I would like to thank the sponsors and their organizations: Barb Szabo (Bell Canada), Colonel Richard Cote Jr. (U.S. Marine Corps), Poul Tonny Kjaer (StatOil), Dean Creed (Santee Cooper) and Bob Marx (U.S. Air Force). Without their desire to improve their organizations, we would not have had the opportunity to learn from their implementations.

CAM-I's Process Based Management team have had many people who have provided guidance as they progressed through this undertaking. Alan Vercio (Bank of America) has been instrumental in providing input and challenging our assumptions. Dean Creed (Santee Cooper) has continually provided us with fresh perspectives and has been the team's eyes and ears on additional materials that needed to be reviewed. Jens Kristian Elkjaer-Larsen (Copenhagen School of Business) was willing to share his research from Scandinavian organizations and debated the merits of various approaches to process based management.

Many individuals took the time to review and comment on what has been captured in committing this to print. I again express appreciation to Alan Vercio (Bank of America), Ashok Vadgama (Motorola), Bill Langdon (Society of Management Accountants of Canada), Tom Freeman (Microsoft) and Barry Brinker (Vanguard Group) for their efforts in providing feedback and insights for consideration and inclusion.

Many others spent time with the project team and provided different insights that were needed to shape the team's collaborative thinking. In particular, they were influenced by Art Schneiderman and Jim Brimson, both of whom have contributed much to Process Management through their writings and insights.

"Process Based Management: A Foundation for Business Excellence" is the result of CAM-I's time-proven collaborative research model that has become the hallmark of the Cost Management Systems program. As Program Director I take a great deal of pride in seeing the integrity of our research forum underwriting the quality of this deliverable from inception. This work is truly the product of many minds working together in providing collective insights to help organizations as they move along the road to becoming process-based.

Ron Bleeker
Cost Management Systems Program Director
CAM-I

TABLE OF CONTENTS

Process Based Management: A Foundation for Business Excellence

Chapter 1– INTRODUCTION TO THIS BOOK

Section 1: Process Based Management

Chapter 2 – WHAT IS PROCESS BASED MANAGEMENT

Chapter 3 – THE BENEFITS OF PROCESS BASED MANAGEMENT

Section 2: The Process Based Management Loop

Chapter 4 – DISCIPLINE MODEL

Chapter 5 – ASSESSMENT FRAMEWORK AND CASE STUDY FINDINGS

Chapter 6 – THE PROCESS CONTINUUM MODEL

Section 3: Key Learning's and Fitting it all Together

Chapter 7 – KEY LEARNING'S FROM THE CASE STUDIES

Chapter 8 – FITTING IT ALL TOGETHER

Appendices

A. Glossary

B. Case Study Summaries

C. Bibliography

Index

TABLE OF FIGURES AND EXHIBITS

Chapter 6

Chapter 7

Chapter 8

CHAPTER 1:

INTRODUCTION

In today's business environment, organizations are experiencing pain they can no longer ignore:

- The delivery of products and services need to continuously improve to meet customer expectations
- A need to reduce time-to-market for products and services.
- Process-focused initiatives that are poorly linked to one another:
  - Examples include: ISO 9000:2000, Malcolm Baldrige, Six Sigma, Lean, time-based management, Scorecarding, activity-based management, etc.
- Customer needs and expectations that require continuous improvement to the way organizations operate.
- Aggressive financial targets.
- A need to reduce waste and nonvalue-added activities to remain competitive.
- Downward price pressure.
- Government mandates for change:
  - Government Performance and Results Act of 1993

- Office of Management and Budget A-11 Cohen
  Amendment 1996
- Section 404 of Sarbanes-Oxley

It is imperative that organizations challenge existing practices and evolve in ways that address these pressures. Organizations need a roadmap on how to address these issues in a coordinated and integrated approach. They need insight into an evolving management approach that focuses on the processes in an organization in a holistic manner to improve both customer service and the efficiency and effectiveness of the organization. We call that model Process Based Management.

This book expands on the nature and benefits of Process Based Management and presents some fundamental models that organizations can use to identify gaps in their process-based efforts. The models provide characteristics and attributes that would be seen as an organization progresses along the road to becoming a process-based organization. But first some background on the research and efforts that led to the development of these models.

1.1 BACKGROUND

In the 1997 book The Road to Excellence – Becoming a Process-Based Company[1], the CAM-I Process Management

---

[1] Daly, Dennis and Tom Freeman, *The Road to Excellence: Becoming a Process-Based Company*, Bedford, Texas: Consortium for Advanced Manufacturing-International, 1997.

Interest Group examined various organizations and their approach to implementing Process Based Management. The different methods and approaches from these organizations led to the development of a Process Based Management Framework. This "framework" serves as the foundation for the ensuing work covered in this book.

A key item identified in The Road to Excellence and the underlying research was the need for an evaluation and validation of the framework, utilizing other companies that were not part of the original work. To accomplish that objective, a case study approach with a standard set of criteria was used to determine if the framework was valid and would apply to companies in distinctly different industries.

This case study approach included an assessment, feedback presentation, and discussion of the next steps the company could consider to progress on the road to becoming a process-based organization. The companies were amazed at the depth of knowledge the case study team was able to gain during the effort, which indicates that the assessment criteria are extremely comprehensive.

To ensure that the results from each case study could be compared with one another, each study was conducted using the same set of criteria, evaluated using the same scale, and followed the same process.

Five different organizations from the United States, Canada, and Europe participated in the case studies representing the following industries:

- Telecommunications
- Government
- Utility
- Aerospace
- Petroleum

The decision to look at only five organizations was based on the recurring themes from the initial organizations. As additional organizations were evaluated, the same pattern of findings began to emerge, leading to the conclusion that additional studies would yield similar results.

By assessing organizations at different points in the implementation of Process Based Management, the effort could determine if there would be significant differences in the findings. The following were the situations encountered in the case study organizations:

- "Reengineering" had been completed and deemed a success, but customer service was negatively impacted.
- Design of an integrated customer inquiry process and enabling technology had been implemented, but focus on other processes had diminished.
- Extensive efforts to develop a comprehensive transition plan for Activity Based Management with

detailed action items had been completed, but top management support was lacking to move the effort forward.

- A process to manage a supply chain had been implemented, and the organizations were interested in an independent evaluation of their efforts.

- A new enterprise-wide software package had been implemented, but minimal effort was spent on changing the underlying business processes, resulting in a negative impact on customer service and employee morale.

As the findings showed, there are many potential business reasons to begin the journey to Process Based Management. However, long-term success is limited without an overall strategy for Process Based Management.

With the knowledge gained from the case studies and 3 years of additional Process Based Management research, additional insights and models have been developed to aid an organization's transition to Process Based Management. This book explores those insights and provides details on the models and how to apply them.

1.2 INSIGHTS

An emerging trend in management tools is the convergence of different types of initiatives around Process Based Management, as depicted in Figure 1.1. Most organizations have realized the importance of managing

processes, and have deployed various initiatives to improve
their processes.

Figure 1.1 Convergence of Initiatives

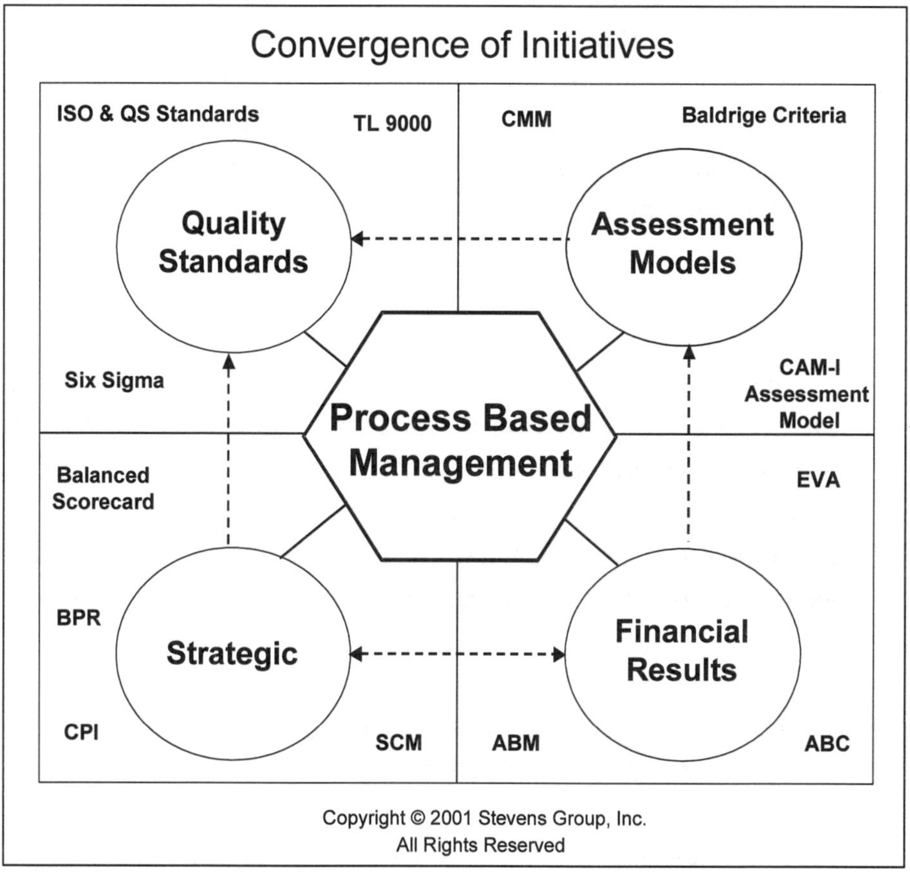

Note: all terms in the figure are defined in the
glossary

These initiatives have been viewed in the past as separate
and distinct, typically deployed independent of one another.

That is beginning to change. Look at what has taken place over the past few years:

- ISO 9000:2000 standard has incorporated customer satisfaction, process understanding and an improvement / assessment approach.
- Baldrige has moved toward "value creation" processes.
- Balanced Scorecard has one perspective focused entirely on processes.
- Six Sigma has come to the forefront as a way to improve process performance.
- Activity Based Management (ABM) is integrating activity based costing with process understanding and improvement.
- Supply Chain Management (SCM) is seen as a critical process for organizations to manage.

To enable the integration of these initiatives, Process Based Management must be viewed as a long-term management strategy, not a tactical tool. While this convergence is subtle to most, we view the use of Process Based Management as the strategic approach to managing and integrating these initiatives, which enables an organization to focus on changing the mindset instead of implementing independent initiatives.

1.3 MODELS FOR PROCESS BASED MANAGEMENT

What was apparent from our research and case studies

was that many organizations have no mechanism to address the convergence of initiatives from a management perspective. Nor do they have a way to assess how they are doing as they progress along the journey to becoming process-based. The research indicated the need for a:

- Way to communicate the strategic view of Process Based Management
- Means to evaluate the management approach of an organization
- Method to determine the level of maturity of Process Based Management in an organization

To address these needs, we developed the "Process Based Management Loop" – Figure 1.2. This loop is the foundation for assessing an organization's process-based efforts and provides a conceptual structure showing how the different models interact.

Figure 1.2 Process Based Management Loop

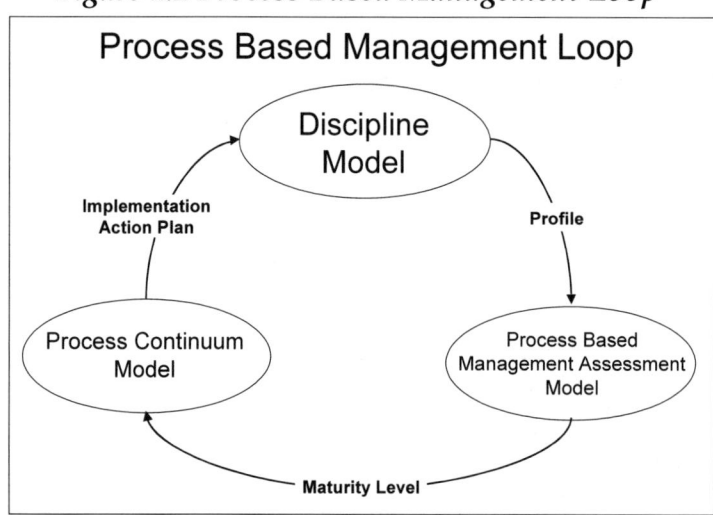

The first model in the Loop is the **Discipline Model**. The Discipline model is a conceptual framework that an organization would use to gain an understanding of how their tools, methods, and initiatives support the business model and their overall management philosophy. This linkage to a management philosophy will enable an organization to select and implement the appropriate methods and tools to support their specific business direction and strategy. Figure 1.3 provides a visual depiction of the Discipline Model.

Figure 1.3 Discipline Model

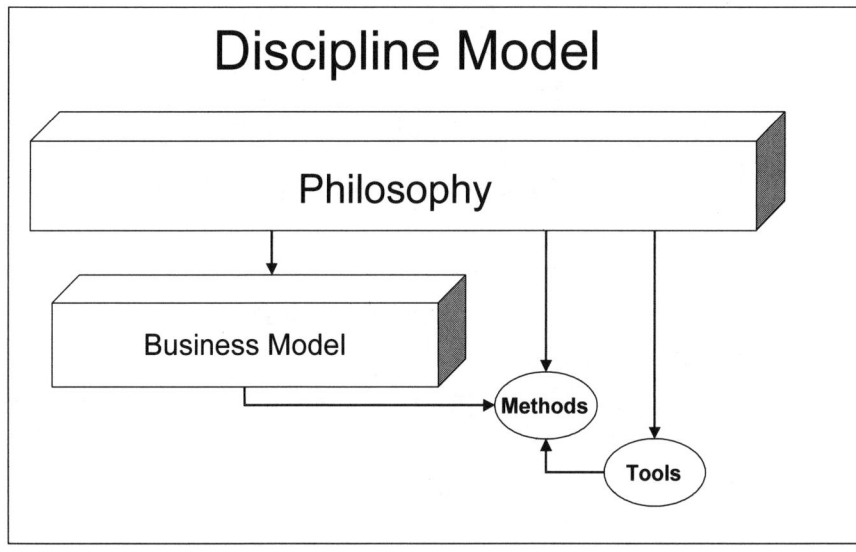

There are four levels to the Discipline model, summarized as:

- *Philosophy* - A systematic way of thinking and doing. It permeates an organization. Everything the organization does and considers is impacted by the philosophy and does not change often. The Philosophy includes the vision, mission, values and management approach of the organization.
- *Business Model* - Includes the strategy, operating plans, and related initiatives that are developed to implement the strategy. This is the framework for identifying how your business creates, delivers, and extracts value.
- *Methods* - Defines the methods used in the organization to execute the strategy and support the direction provided by the philosophy. These methods could be viewed as laying out the steps required to implement initiatives and are typically recognized methodologies that have well-developed and time-tested steps.
- *Tools* - Provides support for the methods. These are the specific devices used. The tools are required for the methods to be successful. **Tools are the enablers, not the drivers, of change**.

By working through the different levels in the Discipline Model, an organization can develop a profile depicting how its philosophy, business model, methods, and tools are currently linked and deployed. The profile will also indicate the history of these initiatives in the organization.

For process-based organizations, the profile will identify the entry point for Process Based Management in the organization, which is key to understanding how the organization got to where it is now. With the profile created, the next step is to evaluate how well Process Based Management has been implemented and identify any gaps that require additional efforts.

This brings us to the next model in our loop, the **Process Based Management Assessment Model** – the framework for the model is shown at Figure 1.4. This model, which has been tested and validated through our research and case studies, provides an overall assessment of an organization's progress in implementing Process Based Management.

Using the categories depicted in Figure 1.4, an organization would work through the assessment process to determine those areas it does well (their strengths) and identify the categories where additional efforts are needed (their gaps). The overall results from the assessment are then evaluated to determine the organization's maturity level in implementing Process Based Management. The maturity level of each of the categories is then used as input into the Process Continuum Model.

Figure 1.4 Process Based Management Assessment Framework

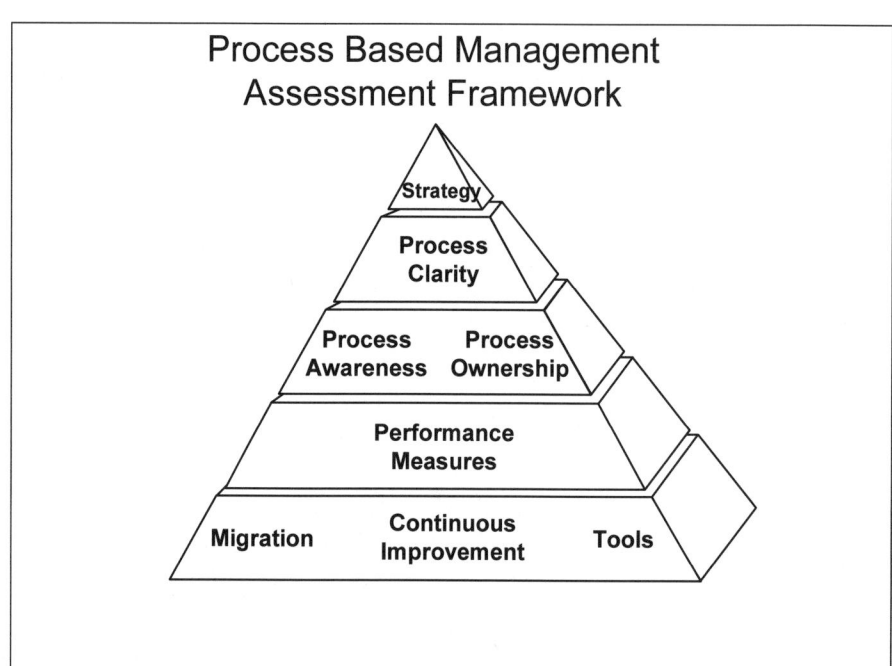

Process Based Management Assessment Framework

© 1999 - Stevens Group, Inc. & CAM-I – All Rights Reserved

The maturity levels lead us to the final model in our loop, the **Process Continuum Model**[2] -Figure 1.5. The Process Continuum Model is a conceptual model that has been developed to identify and capture the characteristics an organization should have, or needs to acquire, during the transformation to Process Based Management. The output

---

[2] The Process Continuum Model is an adaptation of the Metric and Maturity model developed by Texas Instruments. *Metrics: A Management Guide for the Development and Deployment of Strategic Metrics*, Texas Instruments Incorporated, 1997.

from the Process Based Management Assessment Framework would direct an organization to the specific maturity level in the appropriate category to determine what characteristics they would expect to see. This model contains four maturity levels. An example of the characteristics for the Process Clarity category is shown in Figure 1.5.

Using the characteristics for each category, the organization can now develop specific action plans to address any characteristics not currently demonstrated, thus addressing their gaps from the Process Based Management Assessment Framework. The Process Continuum Model can also assist an organization in progressing to the next level of maturity by identifying the characteristics of the next level, which aids in the development of specific action plans to improve their overall Process Based Management maturity.

Once action plans are developed and implemented, the organization would begin the loop again by applying the Discipline Model, thus beginning the iterative process as depicted in Figure 1.2.

Although there is an implied sequence to the Process Based Management Loop, we have found that each of the models can provide value independently. However the collective value of the linked loop outweighs the independent use of the models. Entry into the loop can be from any one of the three models; however progress through the loop is typically clockwise. As you read the book you

Figure 1.5 Process Continuum Model

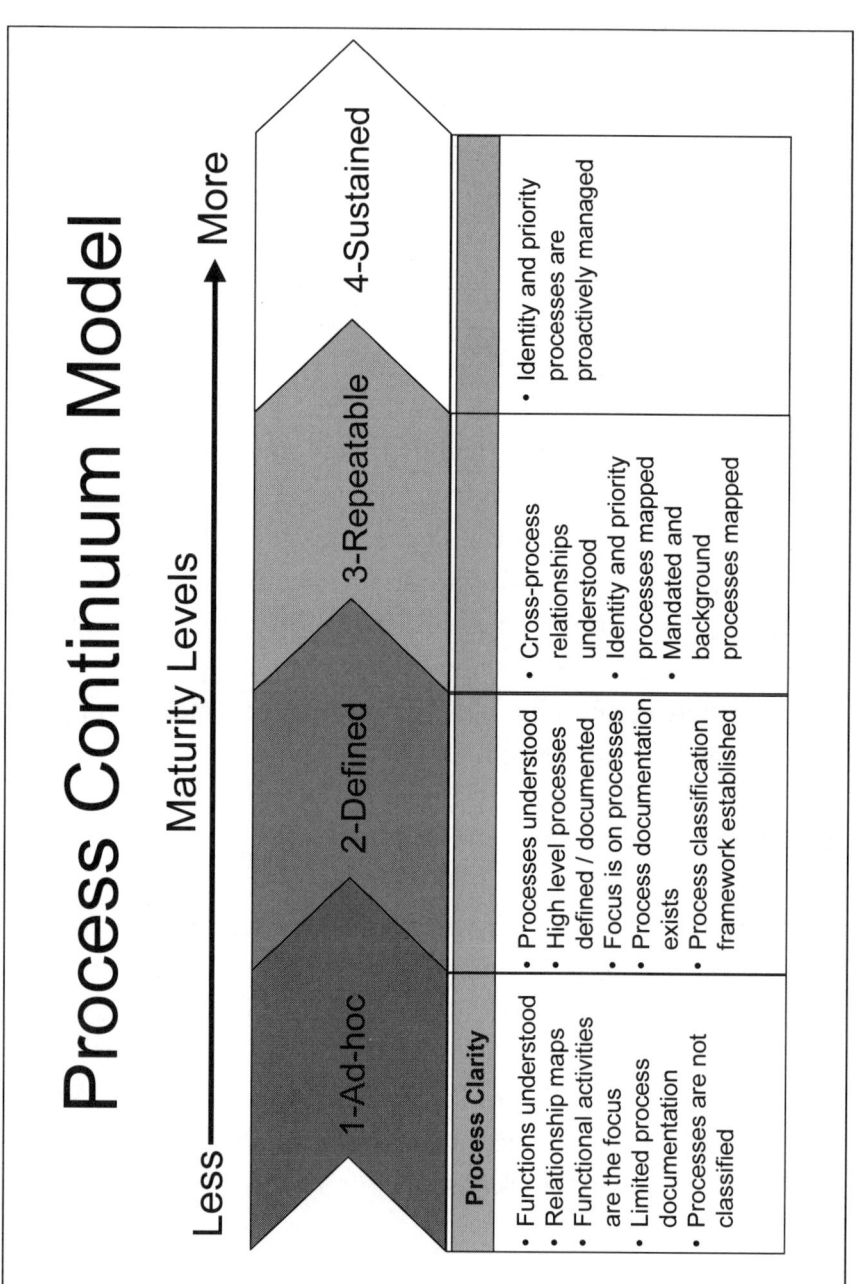

will learn about each of the models and how they interact with one another.

1.4 STRUCTURE OF THE BOOK

The book is divided into four sections and covers the following topics:

- *Section 1 – Process Based Management* sets the foundation by explaining Process Based Management in detail (Chapter 2) and the Benefits of Process Based Management (Chapter 3)

    Chapter 2 explains what Process Based Management is. The approach defined in "The Road to Excellence" has not changed, but the strategic view of Process Based Management is further defined and expanded. We differentiate between managing processes, a key to individual process improvement, and Process Based Management, a holistic view of the enterprise.

    Chapter 3 develops the need to focus on processes and defines the benefits of deploying Process Based Management.

- *Section 2 – Process Based Management Loop*
    The Loop is developed in discussion of the Discipline Model (Chapter 4), Process Based

Management Assessment Framework (Chapter 5)
and Process Continuum Model (Chapter 6)

A challenge of managing any organization is
integrating and controlling all the various
initiatives underway at any point in time. Chapter
4 introduces the Discipline Model, which provides
a framework for evaluating and integrating the
various initiatives, methods and tools in any
organization. This model incorporates the
Philosophy and business model of an organization
as a means of filtering and aligning what needs to
occur in the organization.

Chapter 5 explains the Process Management
Assessment Framework and how it was
developed based on the prior work included in
The Road to Excellence. Most of the chapter
focuses on the case studies and describes the key
observations for each assessment category.

Chapter 6 introduces the Process Continuum
Model, which describes an organization's level of
maturity with Process Based Management and the
characteristics for each level. Each of the 4 levels
(Ad Hoc, Defined, Repeatable, and Sustained) is
defined along with an explanation of the
characteristics for each level.

- *Section 3 – Fitting it all together* summarizes key learning's (Chapter 7) and addresses how to apply (Chapter 8) the Process Based Management Loop.

  Chapter 7 summarizes the key learnings from the case studies and related research.

  Chapter 8 provides a scenario of how an organization would apply the Discipline Model, Process Based Management Assessment Model, and the Process Continuum Model. The results from each model are described, as well as how an organization would use these results in evaluating their efforts toward Process Based Management.

- *Appendices - Case study summaries*
  We provide an executive summary of the five cases conducted, along with our assessment of where they were on The Road to Excellence using the Texas Instrument's 'Process and Metrics Maturity Model'[3].

---

[3] Texas Instruments, *Metrics: A Management Guide for the Development and Deployment of Strategic Metrics*, 1996. p.12.

SECTION 1

PROCESS BASED MANAGEMENT

Process Based Management sets the foundation by explaining Process Based Management in detail (Chapter 2). The chapter builds from managing a process to managing a portfolio of processes. The various facets of the Process Based Management approach are then introduced. This section concludes with a discussion of the benefits to an organization of Process Based Management (Chapter 3).

CHAPTER 2:

WHAT IS PROCESS BASED MANAGEMENT?

OBJECTIVES:

1) Describe the difference between managing a process, managing a portfolio of processes, and a holistic approach called Process Based Management.

2) Describe the facets of a Process Based Management approach

All organizations provide products or services to customers through cross-functional business processes. Yet many organizations do not understand or manage these processes. Our premise is that an organization that focuses on managing these processes will achieve greater customer satisfaction and outperform their competitors.

A process can be understood as a value chain, where each step adds value to the preceding step (as measured by its contribution to the creation or delivery of a product or service). Business processes are the essential view that spans functional boundaries, linking together employees, management capabilities, and technologies to enable an organization to focus its strategy to increase value to its customers. In fact, business process understanding begins and ends with an external customer. Business processes are differentiated from work processes. Work processes are those activities that are entirely within the control of a single department. Process Based Management involves the explicit recognition and management of the businesses' processes undertaken to meet, or exceed, an organization's stakeholders' needs.[4]

How does a process-focused organization outperform its competitors and increase value to the customer? These organizations understand, measure, and continuously improve its processes using Process Based Management as the approach. The reality is that processes are the key ingredient to organizational effectiveness and efficiency.

Louis V. Gerstner, jr., former CEO of IBM states:

"Execution – getting the task done, making it happen – is the most unappreciated skill of an effective business leader. In my years as a consultant, I participated in the development of many strategies for many companies. I will

---

[4] Daly, Dennis C. and Tom Freeman, *The Road to Excellence: Becoming a Process-Based Company*, Bedford, Texas: Consortium for Advanced Manufacturing-International 1997, p. 16-17.

let you in on a dirty little secret of consulting: It is extremely difficult to develop a unique strategy for a company; and if the strategy is truly different from what others in the industry are doing, it is probably highly risky. The reason for this is that industries are defined and bounded by economic models, explicit customer expectations, and competitive structures that are known to all and impossible to change in a short period of time.

Thus, it is very hard to develop a unique strategy, and even harder, should you develop one, to keep it proprietary. Sometimes a company does have a unique cost advantage or a unique patented position. Brand position can also be a powerful competitive position – a special advantage that competitors strive to match. However, these advantages are rarely permanent barriers to others.

At the end of the day, more often than not, every competitor basically fights with the same weapons. In most industries five or six success factors that drive performance can be identified. For example, everyone knows that product selection, brand image, and real estate costs are critical in the retailing industry. It is difficult, if not impossible, to redefine what it takes to be successful in that industry. Dot-com retailers were a good example of a spectacular failure to understand that you cannot suspend the fundamentals of an industry

So, execution is really the critical part of a successful strategy. Getting it done, getting it done right, getting it done better that the next person is far more important than dreaming up new visions of the future.

All of the great companies in the world out-execute their competitors day in and day out in the marketplace, in their manufacturing plants, in their logistics, in their inventory turns---in just about everything they do. Rarely do great companies have a proprietary position that insulates them from the constant hand-to-hand combat of competition.'[5]

"The best companies in an industry build processes that allow them to outperform their competitor's vis-à-vis these success factors. Think about great companies: Wal-Mart has superb processes in store management, inventory, selection and pricing. GE is world-class in cost management and quality. Toyota is best in class in product lifecycle management.

Great companies cannot be built on processes alone. But believe me, if your company has antiquated, disconnected, slow-moving processes---particularly those that drive success in your industry---you will end up a loser."[6]

---

[5] Gerstner, Jr., Louis V., *Who Says Elephants Can't Dance? Inside IBM's Historic Turnaround*, New York, NY: HarperCollins Publishing 2002, p.228-229.

[6] Gerstner, Jr., Louis V., *Who Says Elephants Can't Dance? Inside IBM's Historic Turnaround*, New York, NY: HarperCollins Publishing 2002, p.232.

Process Based management is an approach that governs the mindset and actions in an organization. It is a philosophy of how an organization manages its operations. It is aligned with, and supported by, the vision, mission and values of the organization. It is the basis on which decisions are made and actions are taken.

Process Based Management has a wider scope than just managing individual processes. A process-based organization explicitly recognizes that it will manage and operate all processes to balance and optimize the delivery of value to the customer. The organization is using Process Based Management as a strategy to differentiate itself and outperform its competitors. However, as the strategy is updated and evolves in reaction to changes in the business environment, the process focus remains embedded in the mindset and philosophy of the organization. The strategy is continually influenced and directed by this philosophy.

2.1 MANAGING INDEPENDENT PROCESSES

The movement toward Process Based Management inevitably starts in most organizations by managing a few processes. Processes need to be managed since they focus on "how things happen" and "how to make things happen." There is tremendous value to managing each independent process; this is how a process is continuously improved. Figure 2.1 shows how an order fulfillment process would be managed. As departments work together, employees are engaged as process performers on process teams, many of

Figure 2.1 Order Fulfillment Process

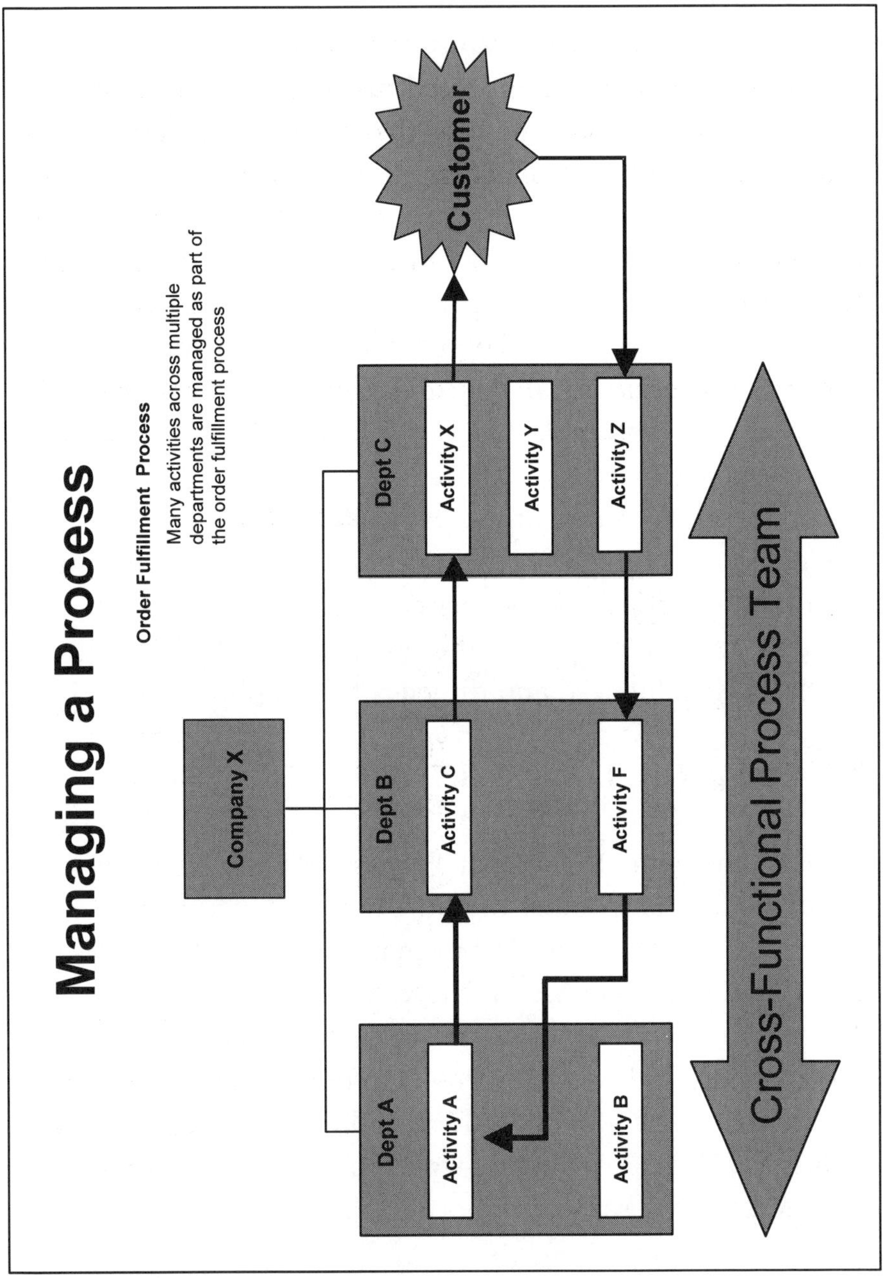

them thinking cross-functionally for the first time. Instead of just thinking about their job, each member of the process team is now thinking about how the process provides products and services, and value, to the customer.

By managing independent processes similar to order fulfillment, an organization realizes the value of improving and managing a process. It sees process measures in action, and how these measures impact the behavior of the process performers, and the resulting performance of the process. Management also sees the limitations of managing processes independently. It looks for an approach to manage the portfolio of business processes to improve value to the customer. As management recognizes that the external customer is the beginning and end of every process, the organization is prepared to start on the journey to becoming a process-based company.

With individual processes being managed and an increasing focus on the customer, these independent processes are brought together and become an integrated and conscious part of management's thinking. The organization shifts to managing the "white space"[7] between independent processes in order to:

---

[7] "White space" is a term adopted from Rummler, Geary A. and Alan P. Brache, *Improving Performance: How to Manage the White Space on the Organization Chart*, 2nd Edition, San Francisco, CA: Jossey-Bass Publishers, 1995. The white space is the critical interfaces between processes.

- Eliminate sub optimization, which can occur when one process is improved without considering the effect on other processes.
- Target the right areas for improvement.
- Align all processes and measures to optimize performance.

2.2 MANAGING MULTIPLE PROCESSES

Managing the white space between processes requires a more integrated approach to managing all the processes in the organization. The portfolio of processes can be viewed as a holistic system of interdependencies. Each process in the portfolio needs to be individually managed; however, each process in the portfolio also needs to be managed as a piece of the whole.

This holistic approach requires an organization to identify and understand the structure and relationship of its processes. A hierarchical model, or classification system, is used to prioritize processes for management focus and improvement. It allows an organization to focus on what processes really add value to the customer. Typically, an organization will be able to identify several levels of process hierarchy. Identifying a meaningful process hierarchy requires a good deal of analysis, and is likely to be an iterative process.[8]

---

[8]Daly, Dennis C. and Tom Freeman, *The Road to Excellence: Becoming a Process-Based Company*, Bedford, Texas: Consortium for Advanced Manufacturing-International 1997, p. 31-32.

A frequently used term for the first level of a process hierarchy is a "core' process. What are core processes? Core processes are the essential top-level business processes that are designed to meet customer needs. Core processes span functional boundaries as depicted in Figure 2.1. A second level in a process hierarchy refers to "major" processes. Major processes are defined as processes that support a core process. [9]

A more insightful descriptive breakdown of a process hierarchy   comes from Peter Keen's "The Process Edge"[10], which divides processes into four categories (Figure 2.2):

- *Identity:* Defines the company for its customers, employees, and other stakeholders.
- *Priority:* Strongly influences how well identity processes are carried out.
- *Mandated*:   Work you are required to do.
- *Background:* Work that needs to be done to support other processes.

As shown in Figure 2.2, Southwest Airlines' identity is based on low cost and on-time air travel for everyone. Their advertising slogan "You are free to fly around the country" reinforces this image. Passengers know what to expect: reasonable, consistent ticket pricing; an easy, friendly check-in process; and flight attendants who create an enjoyable

---

[9] Ibid. p. 36.
[10] Keen, Peter G.W., *The Process Edge: Creating Value Where It Counts.* Boston, MA, Harvard Business School Press, 1997, p.25-28.

Figure 2.2 Classification Framework

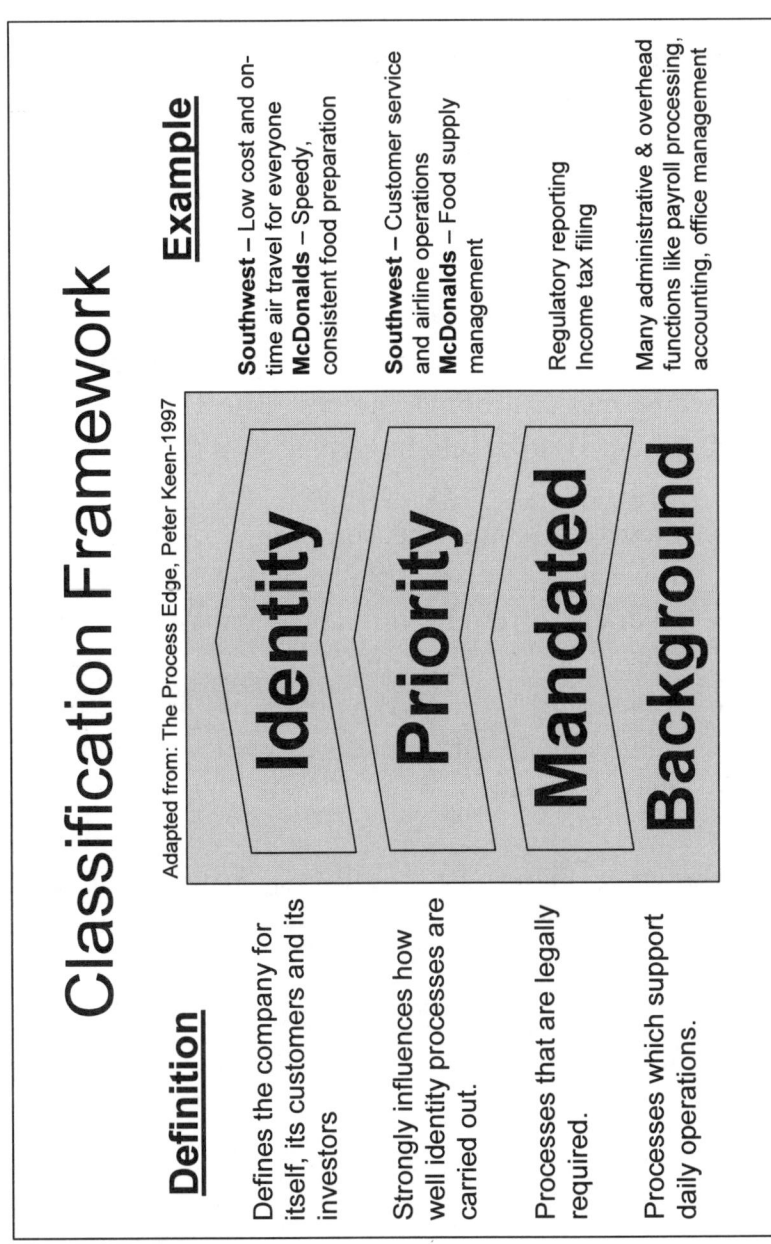

Classification Framework

Adapted from: The Process Edge, Peter Keen-1997

Definition

Identity
Defines the company for itself, its customers and its investors

Priority
Strongly influences how well identity processes are carried out.

Mandated
Processes that are legally required.

Background
Processes which support daily operations.

Example

Identity
Southwest – Low cost and on-time air travel for everyone
McDonalds – Speedy, consistent food preparation

Priority
Southwest – Customer service and airline operations
McDonalds – Food supply management

Mandated
Regulatory reporting
Income tax filing

Background
Many administrative & overhead functions like payroll processing, accounting, office management

flight experience. To make this happen, Southwest is obsessive about customer service, made possible by its hiring process[11] and focus on employee training, as well as excellence in aircraft operations.

Identity and Priority processes have a direct impact on the customer and as a result, are where the organization should focus. Too much time and effort was spent in the 1990s "reengineering" background processes. In most organizations, attention and focus are better spent on Identity and Priority processes to improve customer satisfaction and competitive position. These are the processes that differentiate a company and create competitive advantage. Background processes need to be performed well, but an organization can usually be found that is more efficient at performing these processes. An example is ADP with payroll processing. For ADP, payroll processing is an Identity process; it is how ADP creates value for its customers.

Keen's model is a strategic approach to focus an organization on what is important to the customer. Other frameworks have been developed to classify and organize processes, as well as provide the detail for subprocesses and activities. A widely used framework (shown in figure 2.3) is the American Productivity and Quality Center's (APQC) Process Classification Framework. The approach used in this framework is to break an organization's high-

---

[11] Carbonara, Peter," Hire for Attitude, Train for Skill." *Fast Company*; August/September 1996; page 73

Figure 2.3 APQC Framework

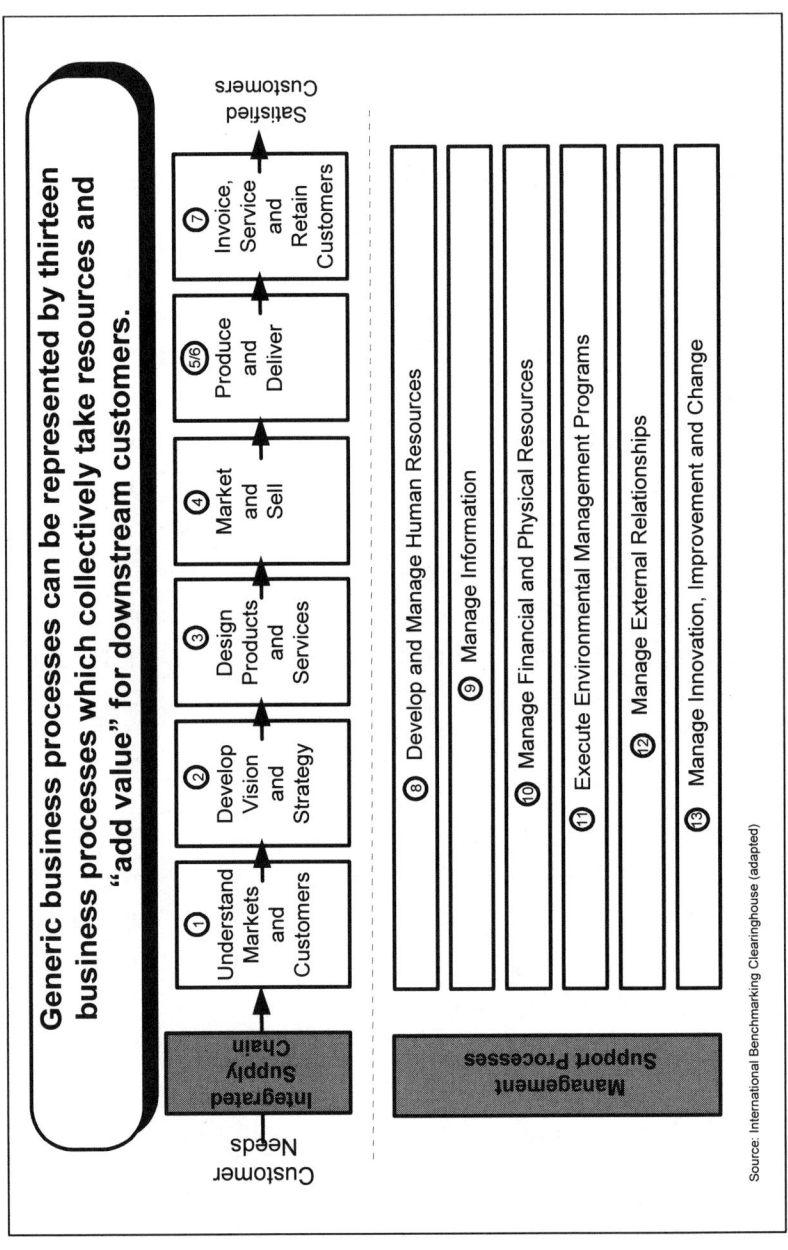

level generic processes into Operating (shown as Integrated Supply Chain) processes, and Management and Support processes. Subprocesses and activities are then provided below each of the generic processes.

Once an organization has classified and prioritized its processes, these processes continue to be managed individually, but also as part of a portfolio of processes. The interrelationships between processes must be explicitly understood, and the organization's processes managed as a system. This can be shown by expanding the Order Fulfillment example to include the complete interaction with the customer, such as in Figure 2.4.

Figure 2.4 Customer Order Processes

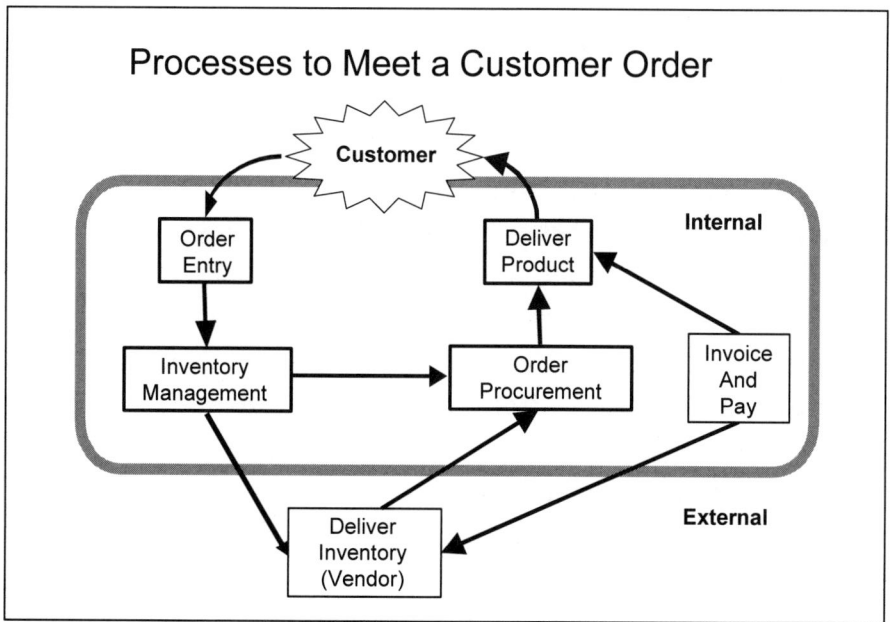

In this example, a customer calls to order a part to be delivered to a specific facility. The customer interacts with the order taker (the Order Entry process) and the delivery person (Deliver Product process). The delivery person could be internal or external (such as FedEx). All the other internal processes, including interaction with processes that are external to the company, are invisible to the customer. However, if all these processes do not work smoothly together, the outcome to the customer will not be satisfactory. Managing each of the processes independently would sub optimize the organization's overall effectiveness. A system is only as strong as its weakest link (or process). Organizations need to coordinate processes so that they can satisfy their customers and accomplish their objectives. The goal of the portfolio approach to managing processes is to optimize the entire system (which addresses the sub optimization issue discussed on page 28).

To optimize an organization's capabilities, the white space between processes must be well managed. This requires that the metrics used to monitor performance are aligned and considered in concert with each other. Each process should be managed using a balance of metrics regarding time, cost, flexibility, and quality. Total system optimization comes from considering all metrics – as a whole set. Tight integration of processes through aligned metrics is the mechanism which allows an organization to meet customer requirements.

Meeting customer requirements must be the goal of each customer interaction. At the holistic level, the portfolio of processes is managed to develop the right processes and the right capabilities to optimize each customer interaction. To do this continually requires that a process mindset be embedded in each employee of the organization.

It is important to note that "organizations are groups of processes and departments or functions. We need to better manage both processes and functions."[12] Organizations have spent decades improving how they manage functions. Now it is time that we focus on improving how we manage processes. As we move from managing a process to managing a portfolio of processes and the white space between processes, we are integrating and embedding process thinking into the mindset of the organization. It begins to become how the organization operates. That is what we call Process Based Management.

2.3 FACETS OF THE PROCESS BASED MANAGEMENT APPROACH

Process Based Management is an approach that focuses on:

- Understanding and meeting customer expectations
- Developing a process-based culture

---

[12] Daly, Dennis C. and Tom Freeman, *The Road to Excellence: Becoming a Process-Based Company*, Bedford, Texas: Consortium for Advanced Manufacturing-International 1997, p.7.

- Managing end-to-end business processes
- Integrating diverse initiatives into a process-oriented approach.
- Linking incentives and compensation to process performance.

Figure 2.5 Process Based Management

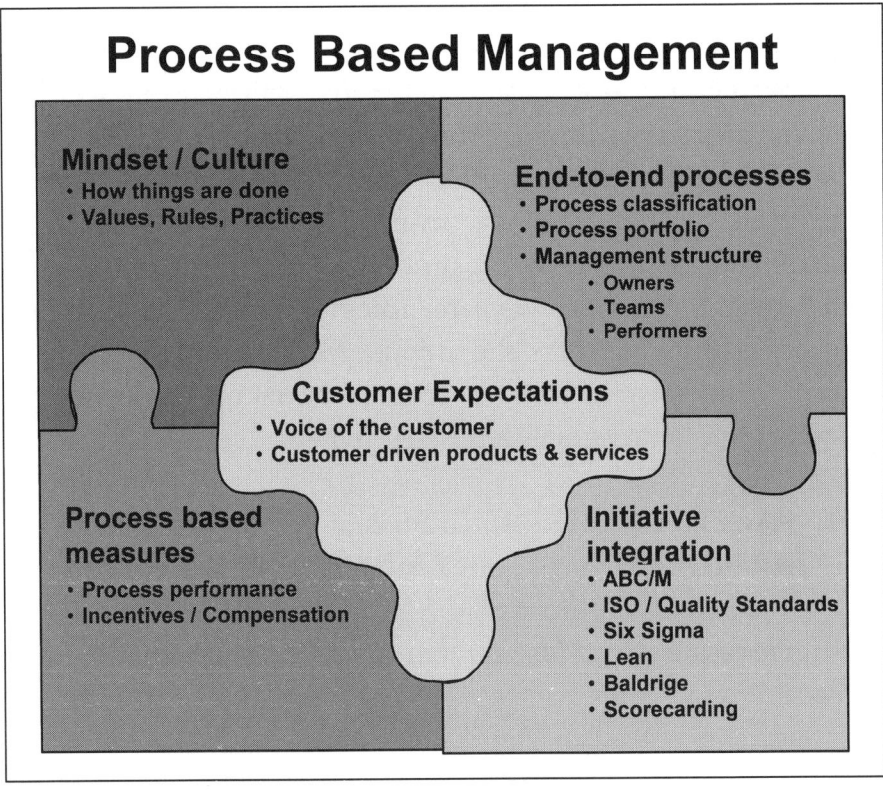

As figure 2.5 shows, Process Based Management builds on the attributes developed when discussing the importance of managing a portfolio of processes. The integrated and holistic aspect of Process Based Management is what embeds this management approach into the philosophy of the organization

2.3.1 UNDERSTANDING AND MEETING CUSTOMER EXPECTATIONS

Organizations need to understand what customers want, and how they value what they receive. The organization can then provide the level of service to meet the customer's specific service expectation, or work with the customer to modify its expectations in line with what can be effectively provided.

There are two separate facets of the customer-value proposition on which an organization must focus. First, an organization needs to understand what a customer values or will value (the voice of the customer[13]). Once the organization understands the customers' needs and expectations, they can incorporate them into the design of their processes.

To accomplish this, the organization needs to have a well-developed process to identify customer needs and desires. Customer needs are often not apparent, and expectations are not always stated. It is imperative that the organization has a process to gather and understand these

---

[13]   Ibid. p.139-141.

needs and expectations. Some organizations use a tool called "quality functional deployment" (QFD) to accomplish this task.

The second aspect is to convert those needs and expectations into products and services that meet those needs and expectations. Those services and products are provided through end-to-end processes. The challenge is to continually incorporate the voice of the customer into the processes that deliver the product and services offerings to meet those needs and expectations.

2.3.2 DEVELOPING A PROCESS-BASED CULTURE

How an organization executes its processes and meets customer expectations is significantly impacted by the culture of the organization. Culture is the environment in which an organization operates. Culture is a mindset (values, rules, practices, rituals, and norms, all of which are frequently unwritten) that permeates an organization and governs how people act. It focuses on how all employees think and approach their jobs. Employees at all levels do not have to think about the culture; it is how things are done. Cultures are not easily or quickly changed. They develop and evolve over time based on the actions of the organization.

Some organizations go to great lengths to instill a desired culture in the organization, and convey that culture in the minds of their customers. When you think about 3M, you picture a culture of innovation and practical solutions. At Apple Computer, the renegade culture was captured in the "Think Different" advertising campaign. Disney creates an image of creativity and family-friendly fun. These organizations link their external advertising to what they emphasize internally in the organization. Inside a process-based organization, a clear, practical awareness of process should be communicated through web sites, briefings, newsletters, and presentations.

At holistic process-based companies, the process culture is embedded in how they operate. The customer focus that is inherent in Process Based Management sets an organization up to succeed in meeting customer expectations. The Dell Business model has been widely diagnosed and written about. The model is centered on building customized computers to specific customer orders, quickly. It is clear that process thinking permeates every business practice at Dell.[14] At Southwest Airlines, process thinking is so ingrained that it doesn't use the term. But every action at Southwest is tied to a process approach; you cannot turn around a plane in 25 minutes[15] if you do not have process teams (including the pilots, flight attendants, and ground personnel) focused on meeting that specific process metric. The result is satisfied customers, timely operations, and low cost.

---

[14] Banham, Russ, "Does Dell Stack Up?" *CFO Magazine Online*, October 1,2003

[15] Southwest Airlines 2003 Form 10K; page A-5

2.3.3 MANAGING END-TO-END BUSINESS PROCESSES

The objective of an effective organization is to continuously improve the time, cost, flexibility, and quality of products and services delivered to customers. The key to the achievement of this objective is an "end-to-end" process perspective. This cross-functional horizontal view focuses on how organizations provide products and services to customers. The objective is to make the complex interactions between internal processes, organizational structures, and tools invisible to the customer through seamless coordination and integration. However, many organizations do not manage their cross-functional processes; as a result, they are not managing how they provide products and services to their customers.

Dell Computer can produce a made-to-order computer and deliver it to a customer within 72 hours. The only way Dell can accomplish this is through a relentless focus on the end-to-end process. So many things can go wrong; however, the only thing that matters to the customer, and to Dell, is that they get their custom-built computer on time. Dell has developed, and continues to evolve, their processes to deliver that value.[16]

---

[16] Park, Andrew with Peter Burrows and bureau reports, "What You Don't Know About Dell," *Business Week*, November 3, 2003, pp.76-84.

2.3.4 INTEGRATING DIVERSE INITIATIVES INTO A PROCESS-ORIENTED APPROACH

In all organizations, there are many diverse initiatives that need to be integrated and aligned to realize their potential value and to optimize their effect on the organization. However, there are usually very few initiatives underway that are linked. All initiatives in an organization should be linked to a management approach and business model in place; for process-based organizations, the initiatives would be linked through Process Based Management.

Figure 2.6 shows some of the many initiatives that could be ongoing at any point in time. Each of these initiatives competes for time and resources. All of them will deliver results if they address a well-defined problem. The dilemma is that most of these initiatives are not linked together and deliver only temporary results.

A common focus of most business initiatives and of the underlying methods and tools that support them is process. Most methods and tools are trying to improve some aspect of a process. Organizations need to link these diverse initiatives with their specific objectives and goals. The linkage occurs as a result of the philosophy in place in the organization and is developed and aligned in the strategy and operating plan. In process-based organizations, that linkage occurs through Process Based Management.

Figure 2.6 Convergence of Initiatives

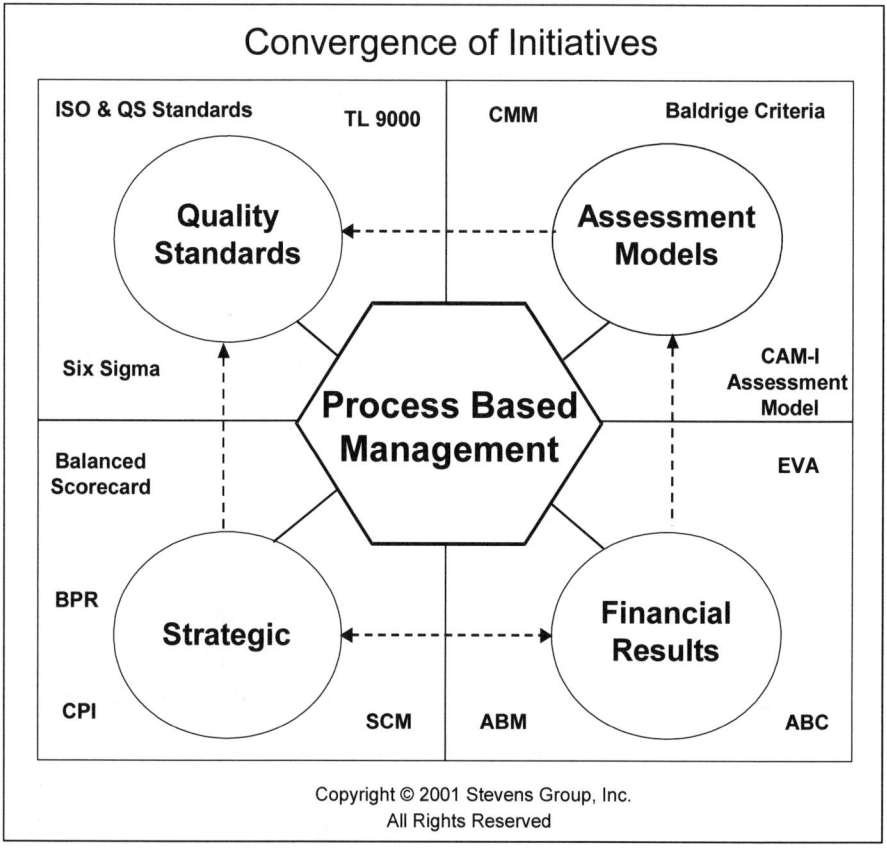

Copyright © 2001 Stevens Group, Inc.
All Rights Reserved

Note: All terms in the figure are defined in the Glossary

2.3.5 LINKING INCENTIVES AND COMPENSATION TO PROCESS PERFORMANCE

A critical component of Process Based Management is the design and implementation of effective performance measures and a complementary performance measurement system. Measurements are derived from the organization's strategy, the relationship of strategy to the organization's stakeholders, the key processes, and the output of those processes.[17] Since processes are how organizations provide products and services to their customers, measures are created for processes so they can be managed.

In process-based organizations, there is recognition that there are employees that: 1) work "**in**" the process, 2) work "**on**" the process, and 3) provide "**governance**" over the process. Each has a different role, and the compensation system recognizes these different roles and responsibilities.

Process measures monitor how the process is performing, and provide insight into the health of the process. Profitability measures are important in measuring the results of the entire enterprise. However, profitability measures are usually far removed by timing and causality from how things happen to have an effect on process performance. Profitability measures tell you what happened, not how things are happening. Therefore, process metrics need to be identified for each key process and aligned between key processes

Effective process measures can be divided into time, cost, flexibility, and quality measures. All of these measures should focus on meeting both internal and external customer

---

[17] Daly, Dennis C. and Tom Freeman, *The Road to Excellence: Becoming a Process-Based Company*, Bedford, Texas: Consortium for Advanced Manufacturing-International 1997, p.110.

expectations[18] and aligned with organizational strategy. These measures need to be simple and easy to understand. For example, the order fulfillment process (Figure 2.1) will have metrics such as the percentage of orders filled correctly, and the percentage of orders filled within 24 hours.

In well-developed processes, the compensation of process owners, process team leaders, and process performers should be tied to these process measures. These process teams are rewarded based on correctly executing, managing and improving the process based on the metrics and targets in place.

Process measures permit an organization to monitor how a process is performing. However it must be recognized that organizations cannot change processes ad hoc. Processes have an acceptable allowance for variability that must be defined by customer expectations and the organizations capabilities. Given this level of acceptable variability, process performers can make decisions. Outside of these control limits, they cannot. Everyone on the process team, for example, understands the importance of these measures, and through a well-defined process, understands their role in achieving those measures.

Returning to the order fulfillment process example, if the percentage of orders filled on time drops from the target of

---

[18] Adapted with modifications from Hronec, Steven M., *Vital Signs: Using Quality, Time, and Cost Performance Measurements to Chart Your Company's Future.* New York: American Management Association 1993, p.18.

98% down to 90%, the process owner and process team should act quickly to determine what is causing the reduction in on-time orders, and then fix the problem. A portion of their compensation is tied to achieving a specific performance level for each measure. In this way, an organization aligns processes to strategy, and guides process performers through clearly defined and understood expectations, with a clear stake in meeting that expectation.

Where do we go next?

This chapter addressed the transition from managing a process to managing a portfolio of processes and the white space between processes. With specific focus on the customer, and the culture, measures and integration in place to manage the end-to-end processes that deliver value to their customers, the organization is implementing a management approach we call Process Based Management.

But why would an organization want to adopt Process Based Management? What are the benefits of this approach? What is wrong with what the organization is doing now? These questions need to be addressed before we can explore in more detail various aspects of Process Based Management.

CHAPTER 3:

THE BENEFITS OF PROCESS BASED MANAGEMENT

OBJECTIVES:

1) Why Organizations should focus on processes

2) Describe the benefits to customers, organizations and employees

3.1 SITUATIONS ENCOUNTERED IN CASE STUDIES

Five case studies were conducted by the CAM-I Process Management Interest Group between 1997 and 2002.[19] The case studies revealed situations in which an organization would benefit from Process Based Management. Some of the situations included:

> ➤ A re-engineering initiative at a telecommunications company cut costs by over $1 billion, but gutted its

---

[19] The CAM-I Process Management Case Studies are summarized in Appendix A to this book.

customer service capability. In addition, the operations division was not in alignment with sales or marketing. As a result, Operations could not deliver the products or services that were being sold. Similarly, a missing link between operations and repairs resulted in frequent customer downtime and physical disconnects within the system. The organization sought to restore quality customer service by focusing on the end-to-end process.

➤ A military organization lacked a process to respond to Congressional inquiries, resulting in lengthy turnaround time and inconsistent responses. The inefficiency of the organization and its customer-facing processes had an impact on Congressional funding decisions. A process was needed to receive inquiries, identify the responsible office, route the request, and track responses to ensure consistency.

➤ An aircraft customer saw a need to describe, define, and link customer service processes to better align with the aircraft supplier. A clear understanding of processes was important to the success of efforts by both ends of the supply chain to better manage and optimize the supply chain relationship.

➤ A utility provider faced with deregulation had a need to refocus on customer needs and expectations. An earlier initiative to improve processes had to be revived and refocused. The approach to examining process across the organization was a significant departure from the organization's historical approach of looking vertically down the organizational structure.

➤ A Scandinavian petroleum company was faced with privatization. Its survival depended on providing world-class customer service, reliable quality, and competitive costing.

These situations and other challenges facing organizations today will benefit from the Process Based Management approach outlined in the previous chapter. These challenges will be addressed first, and then we will explore the benefits from Process Based Management.

3.2 CURRENT CHALLENGES

Organizations are facing unrelenting challenges that are unprecedented in terms of intensity, diversity, and magnitude. Ask yourself which of these pains your organization is feeling:

- The delivery of products and services are not meeting customer expectations
- Constant downward price pressure
- Aggressive financial targets
- Reduction in time to market
- Improvement initiatives that reduce cost but degrade customer service
- Changes in customer needs and expectations require fundamental changes in the way business is conducted

- Failure of Enterprise Resource Planning (ERP) and Customer Relationship Management (CRM) software to deliver on the promise of integration and better business information
- Process-focused initiatives that are poorly linked [5]:
  - ISO 9000-2000, Malcolm Baldrige, Six Sigma
  - Time-based Management
  - Scorecarding
  - Activity-based Management
- Declining industry or market segment
- Market demands to increase efficiency by reducing waste (non-value added activities) and low-value-added activities
- Increased regulatory demands for information transparency – Section 404 of Sarbanes Oxley
- Mandates for change in government:
  - Government Performance and Results Act of 1993
  - Government Management Reform Act of 1994
  - Office of Management and Budget A-11 Cohen Amendment 1996
  - National Defense Panel 1997

---

[5] Adopted from: Daly, Dennis C. and Tom Freeman, *Road to Excellence: Becoming a Process-Based Company*, Bedford, TX: Consortium for Advanced Manufacturing-International, 1997, p.10.

Given this list of challenges that organizations face (and others you could certainly add based on your specific business and industry),_what are the some of the questions that will identify the problems and where to focus?

- Is your organization challenged meeting customer expectations?
- Is your organization (and its internal processes) focused on delivering value to your customers?
- Do you continuously improve how you provide products and services to your customers?
- Do initiatives that compete for resources hinder their effectiveness?
- Do your competitors provide better service to your customers?
- Do your customers consider you easy to do business with?
- Do your employees understand how they provide value to your customers?
- Do your internal communications enable employee empowerment?
- Are employees empowered to improve processes, products and services?

The bigger issue then becomes the possible consequences if these questions and resulting needs are not addressed, such as:

- Reduced customer satisfaction
- Loss of key customers

- Delays in getting products and services to market
- Inability to meet changing customer expectations
- Loss of market leadership position
- Loss of market share
- Employees working at cross purposes
- Inward focus, versus on the customer
- Inconsistent products and services delivered to customers

So how do we address these issues and needs given the management methods and approaches available to organizations today? Process Based Management provides an approach for moving organizations in the right direction to deliver the products and services to meet customer expectations. But how is this different than a functional focus?

3.3 LIMITATIONS OF A FUNCTIONAL FOCUS

Functionally focused organizations are often ineffective and inefficient when work must be coordinated across traditional functional boundaries. This result occurs when the goals of a functional area have priority over the needs of the customer. This creates functional silos and reduces the ability to create customer value. In other words, the customer does not get what they expect. In the extreme, the customer is ignored entirely. "However, work is not accomplished by the structure, but by the processes that flow through the structure."[20] Successful management must be developed and framed within the context of an organization-wide management system, where organizations are managed as groups of processes. They need to be better managed in order to survive and prosper in this business climate.[21]   Figure 3.1 depicts the contrast between the isolation of workflows in functionally oriented organizations and the inclusiveness of workflows in process-based organizations.

This disparity leads to Process Based Management, an evolving management approach that addresses many of the challenges facing organizations today.   Process Based Management is predicated on how organizations provide value to customers, which is through managed and coordinated cross-functional processes. It represents a major and necessary mindset shift in how organizations are managed. It is the vehicle to put strategy into action. "For Michael Dell, inventing the Next Big Thing is not the goal. His mission is to build the Current Big Thing better than anyone else." Dell has won 550 business-process patents. "They're inventing business processes. It's an asset that Dell has that its competitors don't," says Erik Brynjolfsson,

---

[20] Brache, Alan P., *How Organizations Work: Taking a Holistic Approach to Enterprise Health*, New York, NY: John Wiley and Sons, 2002,p.70.
[21] Daly, Dennis C., Dowdle, Pat, McCarty, Bob and Stevens, Jerry, Process-Based Management: The Road to Excellence, *Cost Management*, July/August 2003, p. 12

Figure 3.1 Workflows in Functional and Process-based Organizations

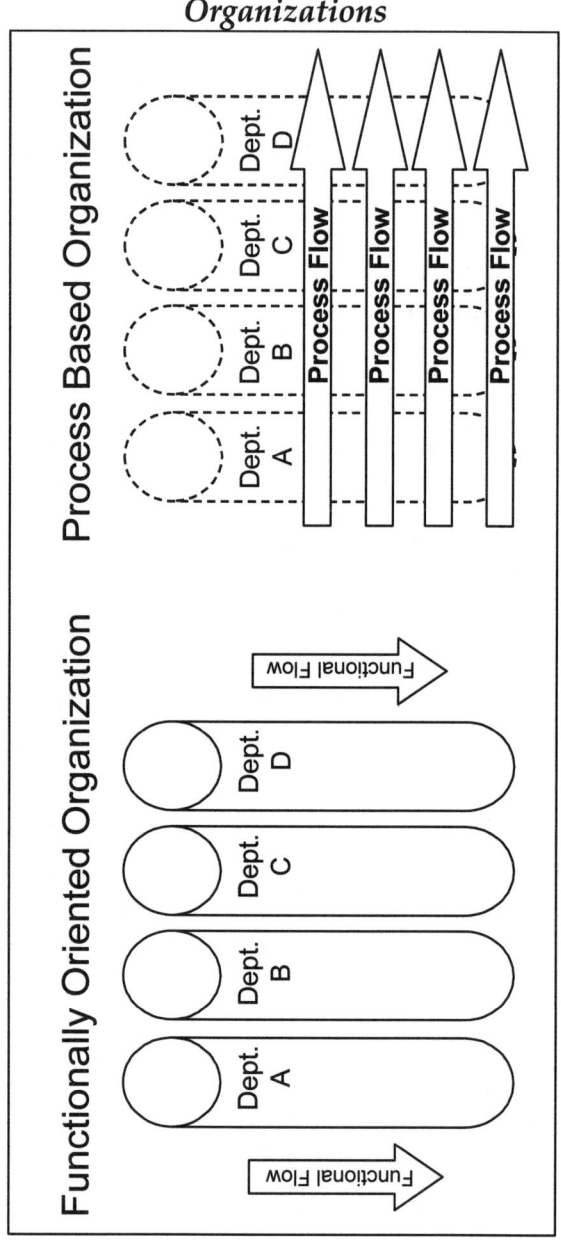

director of the Center for eBusiness at the Massachusetts Institute of Technology's Sloan School of Management."[22]

3.4 THE POWER OF ALIGNMENT AND INTEGRATION

This need to manage processes has not gone unnoticed. Many organizations have adopted methodologies (such as TQM, ABM, scorecarding, and Six Sigma) that focus on managing processes. Each of these methodologies relies on managing processes as their key to success. Yet most of these initiatives do not survive the test of time. Frequently these methodologies accomplish near-term objectives and achieve short-term results, but they are not consistent with the organization's culture or tied to its strategy. Without that link, they do not become ingrained in the organization. In addition, methodologies cannot compensate for ineffective and/or inefficient processes. As a result, they become the "flavor of the month" and are replaced on the agenda by the "next great thing" that comes along. These starts and stops adversely impact organizational effectiveness. Again, the common denominator among these methodologies is that each focuses on processes as the means to achieve its goals; to the extent that this is accomplished, the methodology is effective.

Competing methodologies within an organization can be equally damaging to organizational effectiveness. The damage occurs when departments, functions or process

---

[22] Park, Andrew with Peter Burrows and bureau reports, "What You Don't Know About Dell," *Business Week*, November 3, 2003, p.76-84.

teams adopt different methodologies over time and implements those methodologies independently, causing an unproductive competition for attention and resources. Resources are sub-optimized due to the lack of clarity and a unifying bond around all these tools (Figure 3.2).

Figure 3.2 Competing Organizational Initiatives vs. Coordinated Initiatives

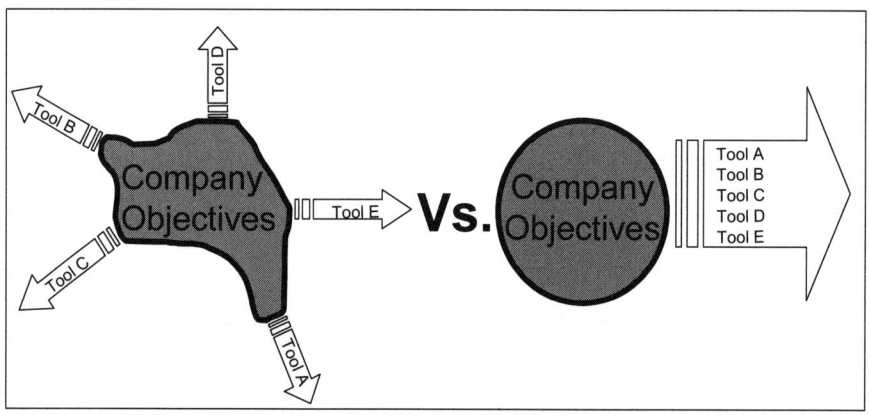

As an example, an organization can adopt Six Sigma in its manufacturing and service areas, Scorecarding for organizational strategy implementation and the Capability Maturity Model (CMM) for software development. However, these methodologies and tools need to be aligned with each other, and with business processes and the strategy to ensure that the organization realizes all of the benefits they offer. When methodologies and tools work together, they support the business model and the philosophy of the organization.

3.5 BENEFITS FROM PROCESS BASED MANAGEMENT

Process Based Management goes beyond managing only a process or managing processes as if they were functions. Process Based Management is dedicated to bringing what often appear to be unrelated activities, functions, processes, and lines of business together to work with a focused mindset toward achieving the organization's strategic goals. (Figure 3.3)

Figure 3.3 Aligning Activities to Accomplish Strategic Goals

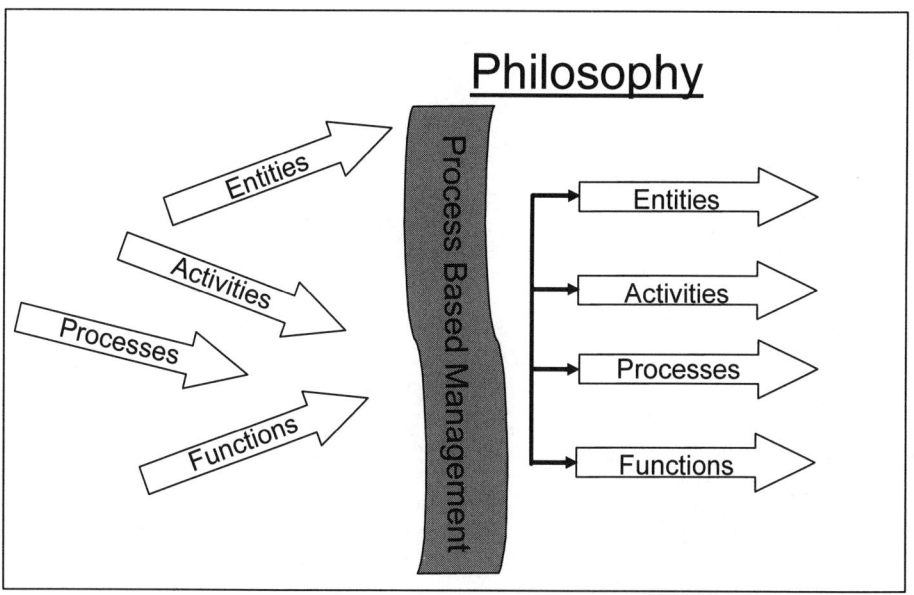

A philosophy and underlying management approach is the driver of how the organization manages and operates. The key is not a specific tool; it is the relentless focus on improving service to customers, which can only occur with a focus on managing end-to-end processes.

Process Based Management creates a unifying strategic mindset to develop value between the customer, the organization and its employees. All are stakeholders in the value chain who reap different, but interconnected benefits. Figure 3.4 summarizes the benefits of Process Based Management.

Figure 3.4 Process Based Management Benefits

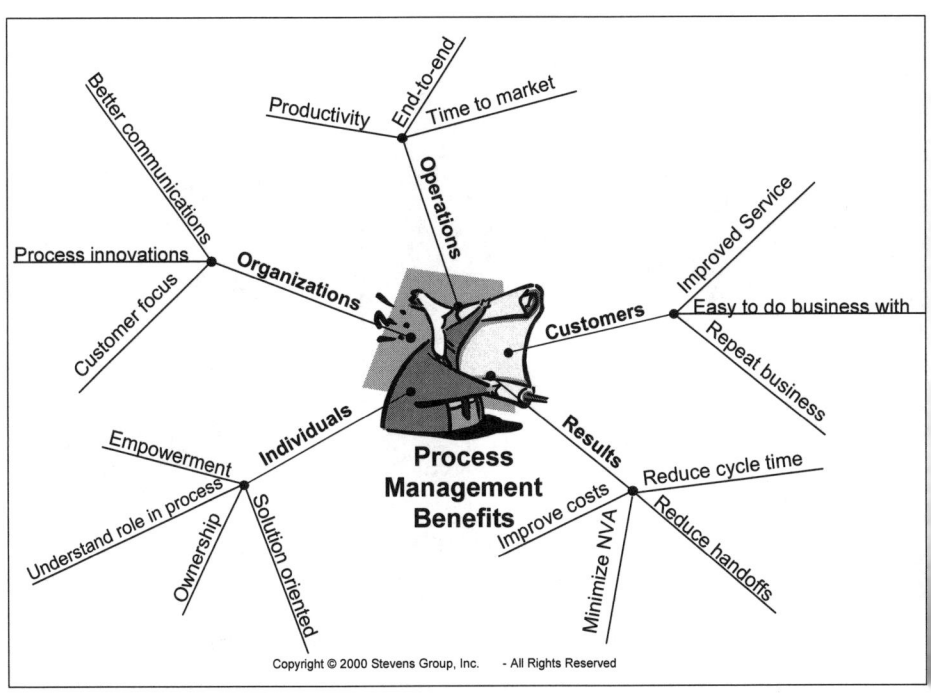

Copyright © 2000 Stevens Group, Inc.   - All Rights Reserved

3.5.1 CUSTOMER BENEFITS

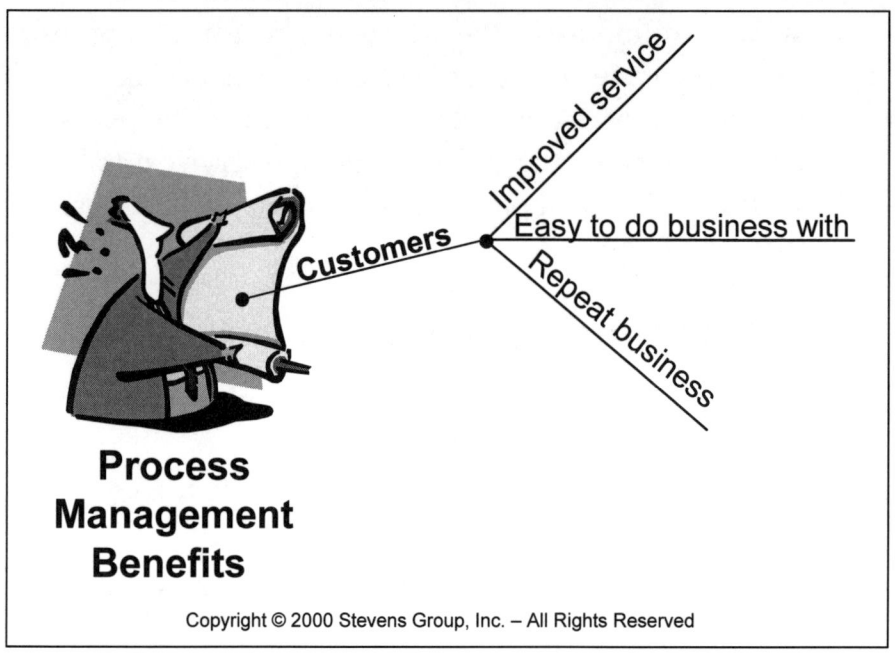

Copyright © 2000 Stevens Group, Inc. – All Rights Reserved

Process-based organizations employ a well-rounded approach to improve service by aligning processes with customer needs and expectations. Meeting customer needs requires making customer focus a routine practice that is most visible as part of the organization's system of measures and continuous improvement efforts.

While negative experiences drive customers away, positive interactions can generate repeat business as customers are attracted by the prospect of continually

improving service, and the increasing ease of conducting
business with the service provider. The customer's exposure
to processes should be as seamless and transparent as
possible. Additionally, the sense of trust resulting from
positive exposure to the organization's business processes
provides an intangible customer benefit. This ongoing
interaction between the customer and the service or product
provider results in an ongoing relationship, or lost business
as shown in Figure 3.5.

Figure 3.5 Interaction between Organization and Customer

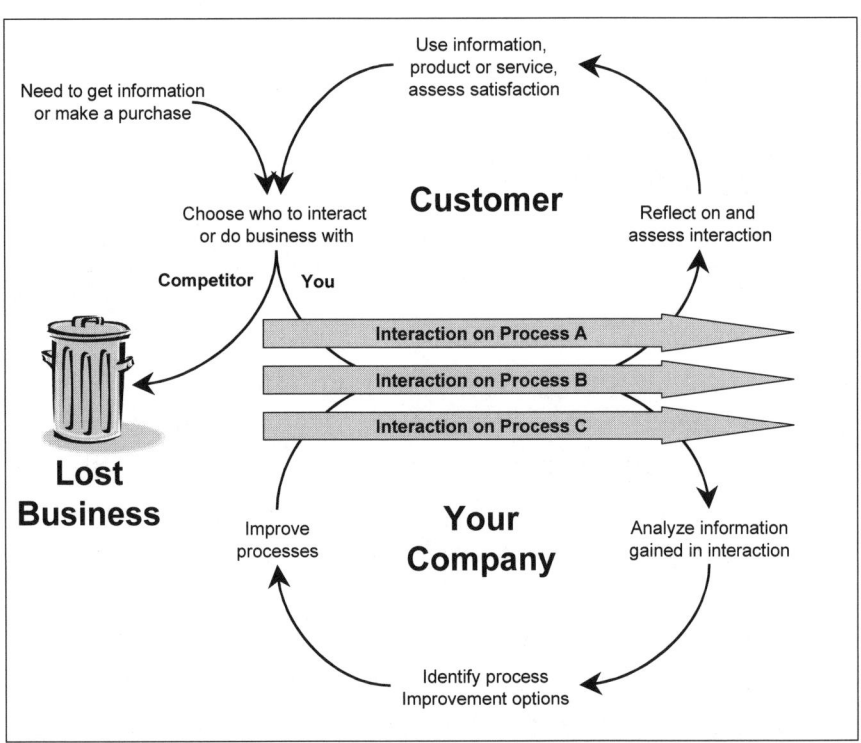

PROGRESSIVE CORPORATION

In recent years, the Progressive Corporation, an automobile insurance provider, has experienced tremendous growth and profitability in an industry plagued by losses and decreasing customer satisfaction. Progressive's remarkable progress can be attributed to its commitment to speed and service when dealing with customers and potential customers. Mobile claim teams operate around the clock to provide a quick response when accidents are reported, and adjusters are empowered to make decisions in the field. These customer-focused processes make use of laptops, innovative software, and wireless communications to allow the adjusters to process claims and issue settlement checks on the spot. As a result, Progressive now measures claims settlement in hours rather than days.

Progressive also uses technology to leverage the process for making insurance inquiries. Customers and potential customers can contact agents, call a toll-free telephone number, or visit Progressive's website to obtain insurance information. In a bold move, Progressive now shares competitors' insurance rates and services with potential customers to enable them to make an educated insurance decision.[23]

---

[23] Salter, Chuck, "Progressive Makes Big Claims" *Fast Company,* Issue #19, November 1998, p.176.

3.5.2 BENEFITS IN OPERATIONS

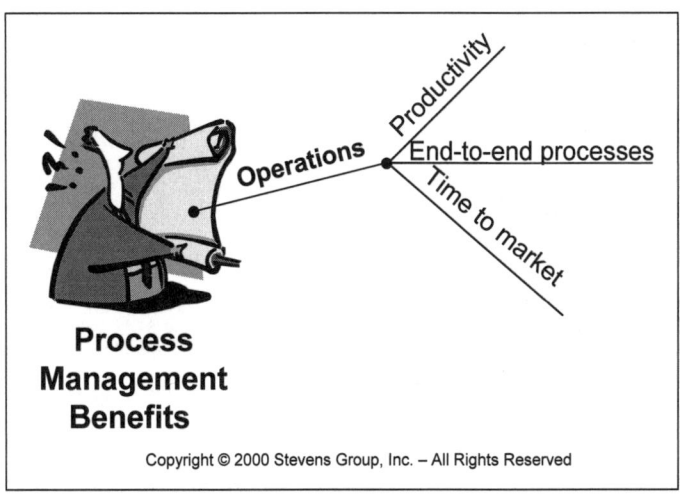

An organization that understands and manages its end-to-end processes is better positioned to achieve desired results, because it is capable of targeting improvement efforts. Looking inward at process capabilities and outward at customer needs are key steps toward meeting customer expectations. Operational benefits in the form of increased productivity and reduced time to market can be realized when process visibility, understanding, and measures reveal improvement opportunities that are then acted on to enhance the process.

DELL COMPUTER

Dell Computer structures its processes around the complete customer experience, which begins when the customer learns about Dell products and continues beyond delivery. To ease the ordering process, Dell established an online ordering process where customers can customize desired computers. Productivity is built around the concept of rapidly delivering reliable, high-quality custom- built computers. In addition to traditional means of gathering feedback, Dell uses teams to monitor Internet forums where customers discuss products. What the teams learn is treated as feedback and used to improve products and processes.[24]

3.5.3 BENEFITS TO THE ORGANIZATION

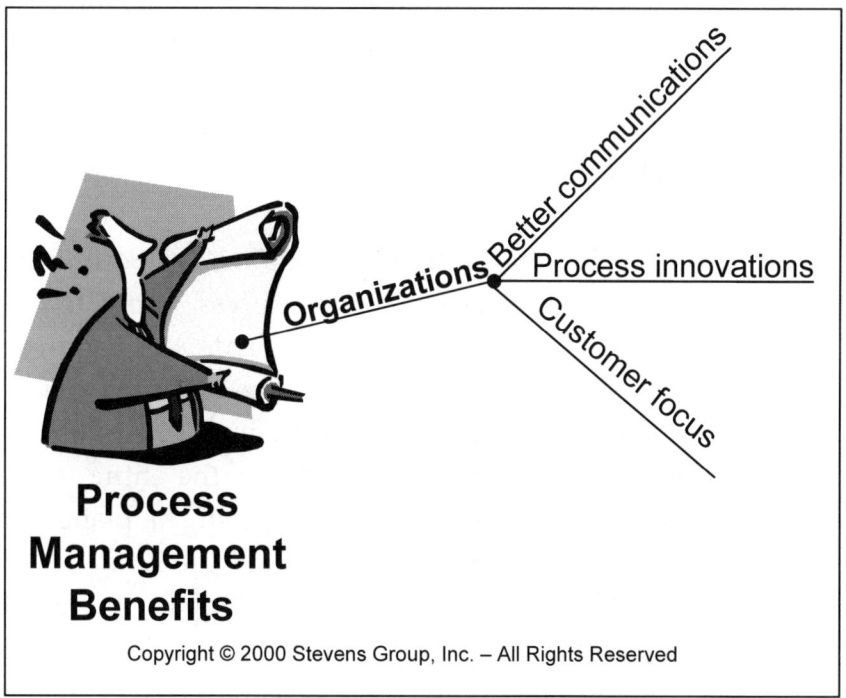

Better communications

Organizations

Process innovations

Customer focus

Process Management Benefits

Copyright © 2000 Stevens Group, Inc. – All Rights Reserved

---

[24] Park, Andrew with Peter Burrows and bureau reports, "What You Don't Know About Dell," *Business Week*, November 3, 2003, p.76-84.

A strong customer focus around its targeted customer segments fosters an improvement mindset that conditions the process-based organization to identify opportunities for improvement. Trying to be all things to all customers will lead to failure; organizations develop their process capabilities based on their targeted customer needs.

Process-based organizations develop and employ broad based communications to articulate improvement plans directed at achieving specific goals. The efficient exchange of customer and process information is vital to the process innovation needed to achieve these goals, and support strategy execution.

SOUTHWEST AIRLINES

In a period of intense industry difficulty, Southwest Airlines has used customer focus and process innovation to grow as others floundered or failed. With a determination to provide its targeted customers spirited, quality service at affordable prices, Southwest Airlines engages all employees in achieving company goals. For example, the entire flight crew is engaged in the process of preparing a plane for departure with the goal of turning around the plane in 25 minutes. In addition to meeting on-time goals, the high utilization of each aircraft avoids costs associated with maintaining a larger fleet. [25] To satisfy customer expectations for an easy way to reach their destinations and return,

---

[25] Southwest Airlines 2003 Form 10k; page A-15

Southwest employs point-to-point scheduling, versus routing flights through hubs.

Southwest responded to customer feedback by creating automated boarding passes to replace the plastic boarding cards issued during check in. The automated passes are conveniently issued at multiple locations within airports and combine the boarding verification process with the former plastic card. Southwest's successful application of Process Based Management techniques has established it as an industry leader.

3.5.4 BENEFITS TO INDIVIDUAL EMPLOYEES

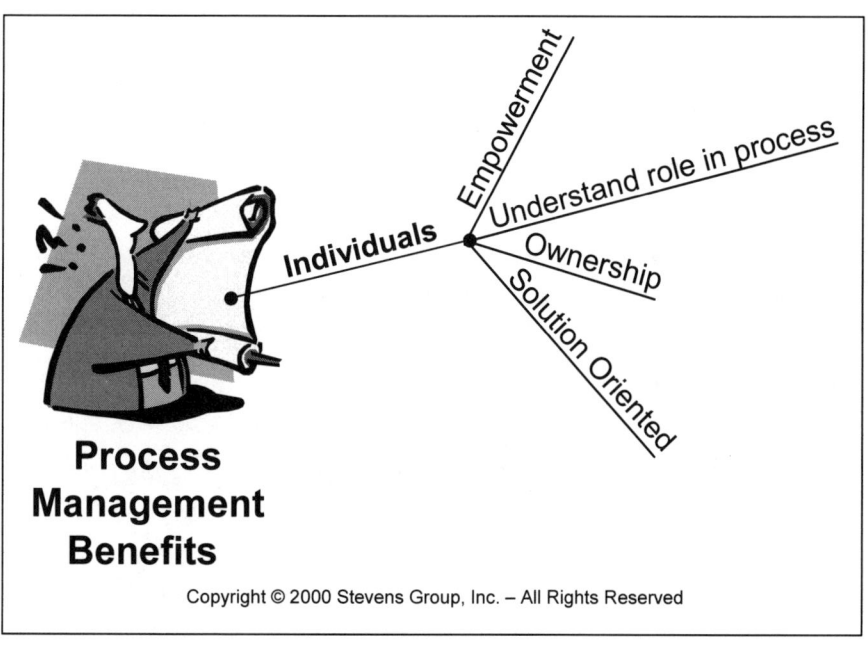

Process Management Benefits

Copyright © 2000 Stevens Group, Inc. – All Rights Reserved

Successfully managing end-to-end processes depends largely on engaging the workforce. From their position as process performers, employees have a perspective management is not readily exposed to. Involving employees in the management and improvement of processes provides critical information and access to the actual mechanics of those processes, the causes of inefficiencies, and the many ideas for improvements.

To engage employees, process teams are formed to manage specific processes. The benefits to the employee arising from process team involvement are many:

- Greater understanding of the business of the organization
- Greater understanding of their role in processes
- Awareness of the impact of their actions on other departments
- Actual empowerment to resolve problems
- Sense of ownership
- Solution-oriented mindset

RITZ CARLTON[26]

The Ritz-Carlton Hotel Company has recognized the importance and benefits of engaging employees in the process of delivering service to customers in their luxury market segment. Before winning the 1999 Baldrige Award,

---

[26] Ritz-Carlton 1999 Baldrige Application. www.nist.gov

Ritz-Carlton experienced nine consecutive years of declining employee turnover, and a 40% increase in revenues between 1995-1999. The company not only encourages employee involvement, it expects it. The Ritz-Carlton employee promise recognizes employees as the most important resource in the company's service commitment. Ritz-Carlton has twenty basic standards that address its approach to service. Four of the standards address employee involvement and empowerment.

Employees are empowered and directed to suspend regular duties to address the needs of hotel guests. To that end, an employee can spend up to $2,000 to immediately correct a problem or complaint. Further, employees do not return to their duties until the issue at hand is resolved, the guest is satisfied, and the situation documented.

Senior leadership also follows a human resources approach directed at increasing employee job satisfaction. The approach involves ensuring that employees know what is required of them, know how well they are performing, and have the authority to make changes. Ritz-Carlton succeeds in this arena by providing extensive and continuous training, providing formal and informal performance feedback and equipping employees with the tools to make change.

In its focus on the customer, a process-based organization continuously strives to meet customer needs and expectations. An advance in one or more of the following common areas positively impacts the products or services delivered to the customer:

- Reduced lead or response time
- Improved first-call resolution
- Reduced handoffs
- Minimized non-value-added activities,
- Reduced service variability

3.5.5 BOTTOM LINE BENEFIT: RESULTS

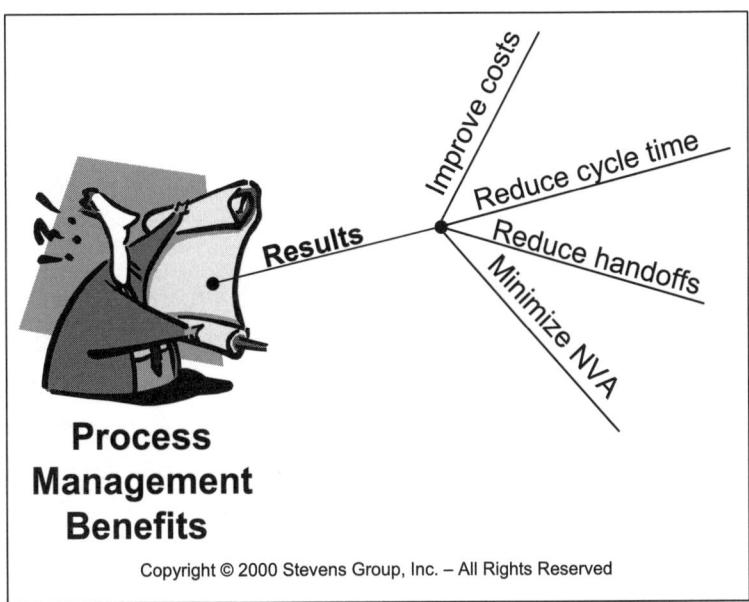

By improving the performance of its processes, organizations are better able to manage the cost of delivering the product or service to the customer. By minimizing the number of handoffs and the non-value-added steps that provide no value to the customer (such as duplicate entry of orders), cycle times can be reduced to meet customer expectations. This also reduces the cost of performing the process, and the resulting cost of the product or service. Continuously improving processes to meet changing customer expectations leads to proactive management of process costs. As the case studies showed, large cost cutting most often leads to decreases in customer service. In most instances, the proactive process approach is a better way.

YELLOW FREIGHT SYSTEMS[27]

Yellow Freight Systems, a company in business for over 70 years, restructured its business processes to adapt to changing customer needs. During the mid 1990's, the company experienced massive losses, two rounds of layoffs and a strike. New management joined the company in 1996 and launched a recovery effort that established the company as an industry leader.

Yellow Freight significantly modified its processes to reduce the handling of freight and to speed deliveries. Technology was used to monitor the location and utilization of trucks, redistribute personnel to load and offload shipments and provide online tracking for customers. Mobile data units put shipping information in the hands of dockworkers and managers. The changes not only put

---

[27] Salter, Chuck, "Fresh Start 2002: On the Road Again", *Fast Company*, Issue 54, January 2002, p.50.

Yellow in a position to provide the customer the flexibility to determine delivery times, but also to guarantee timeliness.

New information systems automatically build customer profiles so that future orders of the same items can be placed in seconds versus minutes. The information feeds a distribution network that has reduced stops, freight transfers and damaged shipments. Company wide, the defect rate has been reduced to 5% and on-time performance exceeds 95%.

3.6 SUMMARY: WHY PROCESS BASED MANAGEMENT?

As Alan P. Brache states in *How Organizations Work*:

"One could argue that a business has only four dimensions:

- Strategy (which defines *what* work should be done).
- Business processes (which define how work should be done).
- Issue resolution (which defines how operational problems are solved, decisions are made, and opportunities are realized as work is being done).
- Leadership (which sees that an energized workforce is pursuing the right strategy, carrying out intelligently designed processes, and efficiently resolving issues)."

"While this 'only four variables' view is too simplistic to diagnose and improve organization health, it does give processes the prominence they deserve. For example, you can have visionary leadership, but if the business processes do not work, the leader does not have vehicles for implementing the vision....

You can have state-of-the-art information systems, but they are only as good as the business processes they support."[28]

Placing the focus squarely on the customer and managing the end-to-end processes, Process Based Management provides a strategic approach to achieve a competitive advantage in the current customer-centric business environment. Dell, Progressive, and Yellow Freight have all followed the strategic approach to achieve their current levels of success.

These organizations have used technology to enhance process capability and to better manage processes. However, their success in implementing technology is the result of their management of processes and the process mindset that exists in these organizations. Without this mindset, technology is most often not as effective at enabling process performance as it could be.

Process Based Management provides different, but linked, benefits to various stakeholders and perspectives of the organization. The key stakeholder is the customer, without whom there is no business; they should see better service and a more targeted value proposition. Moving inward, operations benefits from improved focus and

---

[28] Brache, Alan P., *How Organizations Work: Taking a Holistic Approach to Enterprise Health*, New York, NY: John Wiley and Sons, 2002, p.69.

performance. The people who execute the processes that provide value to the customer, the employees, benefit from the understanding, control and accountability they have as process performers. Shareholders and debt-holders benefit from improved performance. Suppliers benefit from the seamless and transparent interrelationship for lowering transaction costs and improving value to the customer, and the foundation for integrated planning and strategies across the supply chain. Each stakeholder needs to see results: from continually improving products and services to the bottom line impact of better managed and aligned processes.

Process Based Management provides an organization a framework to link discrete initiatives, enabling the organization to improve its focus and customer value on a continual basis. There is wide understanding that isolated initiatives do not lead to sustainable competitive advantage.

That is where we go next. With all the initiatives in place in organizations, there needs to be a way to classify, separate, and prioritize them. Our approach is presented as a Discipline Model.

SECTION 2

THE PROCESS BASED MANAGEMENT LOOP

This section introduces the Process Based Management Loop. This loop is the foundation for assessing an organization's process-based efforts and provides a conceptual structure showing how the three different models to be introduced in this section interact.

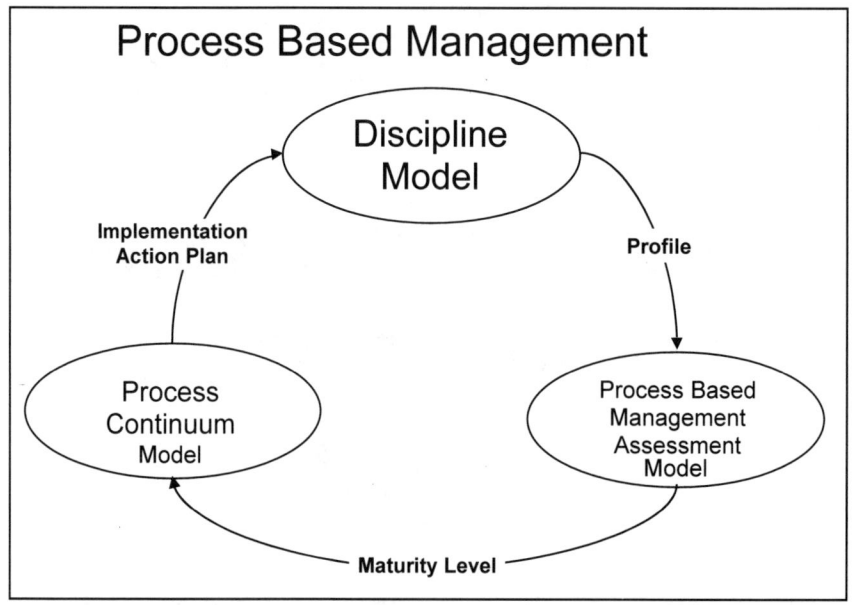

Each of the models will be discussed in separate chapters. We start with the Discipline model.

CHAPTER 4:

DISCIPLINE MODEL

OBJECTIVES:

1) Show the effect disconnected initiatives have on an organization.

2) Present a model that aligns tools and methods to the business model and philosophy of the organization.

3) Provide a framework for an organization to identify its management approach.

Processes are the "how" that puts strategy into action. A focus on process should be central to every organization and ingrained as an essential part of every organization's strategy and culture. The extent to which process is the focus is dependent on the competitive environment and strategy of the organization. In some organizations (for example, Southwest Airlines and Dell Computer), processes are a strategic focus that has resulted in significant competitive advantage for these organizations.

Why is this process mindset not more pervasive? Why are organizations embarking on a variety of independent "flavor of the month" initiatives trying to improve performance? How does an organization link into a process mindset all the various initiatives that are ongoing at any point in time? These are issues that every organization is facing. The starting point is to understand what initiatives are ongoing in an organization, and then to determine how they should be linked.

Initiatives can and do provide benefits, but do not always provide value. A case study company reduced operating costs by over \$1billion, but infuriated its customers. Peter Keen refers to this as the "process paradox."[29] These are the challenges confronting the case study organizations and, indeed, all organizations. To address this paradox and to provide a structure to look at initiatives in organizations led us to develop a framework called the Discipline Model. What became clear as the model was developed was that this model applied not only to process focused organizations, but to all organizations.

4.1 MANAGEMENT METHODOLOGIES AND TOOLS

All organizations have multiple initiatives, methodologies, and tools underway at any point in time. In most instances, before a tool has been fully implemented, provides benefits, and becomes part of the management

---

[29] Keen, Peter G.W., *The Process Edge: Creating Value Where It Counts*, Boston, MA: Harvard Business School Press, 1997, p.3.

system, the next tool comes through the door and the prior tool usage begins to fade away. A Bain study of tools (Management Tools 2001)[30] concluded that on average companies have ten tools in various stages of use in an organization. The Bain study focused on the top 25 tools (Figure 4.1, listed in alphabetical order), but the list of possible tools is endless.

Figure 4.1 Management Tools

Bain Top 25 Management Tools:

- ABM
- Balanced Scorecard
- Benchmarking
- Core Competencies
- Corporate Venturing
- CRM
- Customer Satisfaction
- Customer Segmentation
- Cycle time reduction
- Growth strategies
- Knowledge management
- Market disruption mgmt.
- Merger Integration teams
- Mission/vision statements
- One-to-one marketing
- Outsourcing
- Pay-for-performance
- Real options analysis
- Reengineering
- Scenario planning
- Shareholder value analysis
- Strategic alliances
- Strategic planning
- Supply chain integration
- TQM

Source Bain: Management Tools 2001

Everyone has been in organizations where employees receive guidance on yet another tool, but are never very excited, because they know…'this too shall pass.' Think of

---

[30] *Management Tools 2001: An Executive's Guide,*
www.bain.com/bainweb/publications/Written By_Bain_detail.asp? Article id=5621

the time, resources, energy, and enthusiasm wasted. No wonder there is so much cynicism among employees when a new initiative is introduced.

A "Discipline Model" was developed to provide a context to understand how a tool fits into an organization. The model is broken into multiple sections as shown at Figure 4.2 .

It is important to understand each of the four levels and its relationship to, and interdependency on, the other levels.

Figure 4.2 Discipline Model

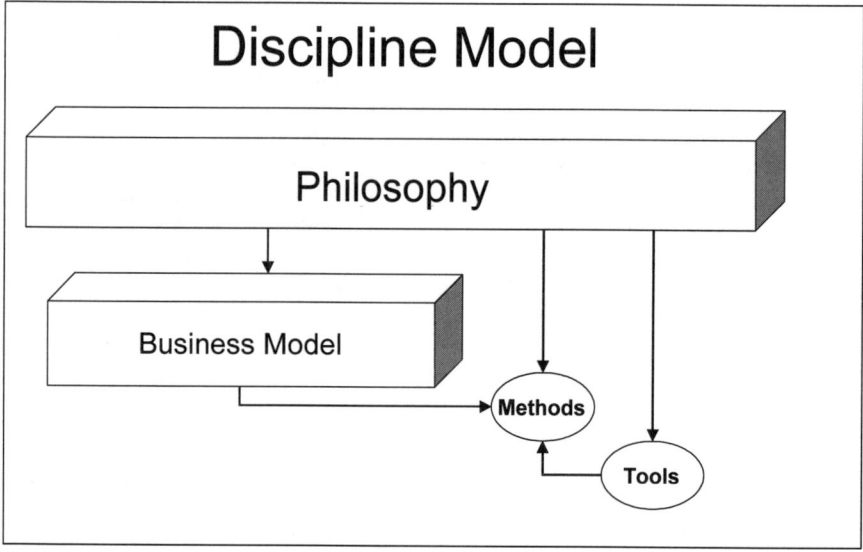

4.2 PHILOSOPHY

At the top of the Discipline model is the philosophy of the organization. A philosophy is a systematic way of thinking and doing. It permeates an organization. Everything the organization does and considers is influenced by the philosophy. It is the bedrock of the organization, and does not change often. The philosophy includes the vision, mission, and values of the organization. It also captures the management approach that is being followed by the organization. In holistic process-based organizations, this management approach would be Process Based Management. A company may utilize aspects of multiple management approaches, but there needs to be an overriding approach that is the driver.

Examples of management approaches followed by organizations would include:

- Process Based Management (Southwest Airlines, Dell Computer)
- Continuous Improvement (Toyota)
- Cost and Resource Management (Emerson Electric)
- Quality (Clarke American)
- Innovation and Entrepreneurial - (3M)
- Brand Management (Procter and Gamble, Disney)

Each of these organizations has used the management approach included in its philosophy as a guide to developing, evolving and implementing its business strategy. Every business must grow and change to survive; what guides this evolution is the organization's philosophy. This bedrock foundation, represented by the vision, mission, and values stays the same, or changes and evolves very slowly, and has a significant influence on the culture of the organization. The management approach also evolves, but the direction and focus stays consistent. A change in the philosophy is a major change. A firmly established philosophy provides the nucleus around which decisions can be made. An organization without an established and communicated philosophy will wander from one idea and approach to another; there is nothing to ground and guide the discussion.

How does a management approach such as Process Based Management become part of the philosophy of an organization? For some start-up organizations, it is embedded from day one as how the organization will operate. The founders recognize this as a management approach which will best help them realize the value proposition for their targeted customers. As such, they set up and structure the philosophy (mission, vision, values, and management approach) of the organization to provide that value. A recent example would include Jet Blue Airlines, which from our observation has relied on a process-based approach as a philosophy to launch the business.

Figure 4.3 Philosophy of an Organization

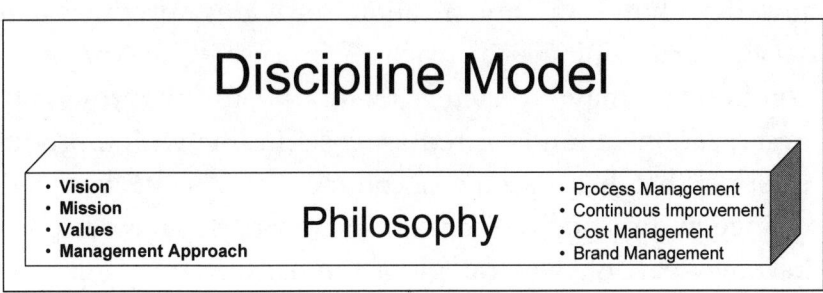

However, most organizations are beyond the startup phase, and have developed "institutional" methods of operating and managing. But the one constant in business is change! Some event or challenge in business conditions will create a need for the organization to change its direction and reevaluate how it operates:

- The loss of a major customer, or a significant new competitor.
- Technology is introduced that transforms product and service offerings, and the entire supply chain.
- Changes in customer needs dictate that the value proposition be updated or radically changed.
- A key, unique product with high margins just became a commodity with low margins.
- Service has become key, and the organization can't quite get it right
- Mergers or acquisitions

How management reacts to these types of events has a direct impact on the longevity and success of the organization. The introduction of a new method or tool to improve how an organization provides products and services can initiate a reactive process. The change in conditions may dictate methods to improve the organization's brand, or reduce costs in line with a product offering that has become a commodity. As the long-term change in direction or focus is developed, this new direction becomes part of the strategy of the organization. Initiatives are developed as part of the operating plan to move toward the new direction. If the organization is persistent and diligent in implementing the strategic direction, it will begin to have success in moving to the new vision and management approach. The mindset at all levels will begin to change as the organization begins to think and act in the new ways management has laid out. Over time, this new mindset becomes how the company operates; the management approach has now become part of the philosophy of the organization.

What this indicates is that a change to the management approach embedded in the philosophy of the organization is not easy; it takes time and a significant dedication and persistence by the management team. It is a major transformation in how a company operates. But sometimes it is necessary. If an organization does not have the right philosophy in place to be competitive in its targeted markets and to provide its intended value to customers, the only alternative to transformation is failure. The struggle of the United States airline industry (in contrast to Southwest) is an example of an industry in need of transformation.

It is essential that all organizations understand what their philosophy is. With that defined Philosophy as the bedrock, there needs to be a level that allows the organization to be adaptable to the ongoing changes in business conditions and the competitive landscape. That level is captured as the business model.

4.3 BUSINESS MODEL

The business model includes the strategy, operating plan, and related initiatives that are developed to implement the strategy. Gary Hamel has stated that a business model is a framework for identifying how your business creates, delivers, and extracts value. [31] An organization needs to understand its business model to know how things should be done. Without this understanding, it is difficult to filter out noise from substance; to know what approaches make sense to the organization and which provide little value based on the philosophy and strategy of the organization. For successful organizations, the business model decisively supports the philosophy and is consistent with the vision, mission, and values captured in the philosophy. A business model that is out of sync with the philosophy will cause chaos and disruption, which leads to failed performance.

IBM in the early 1990s is an example. In 1993, Lou Gerstner took charge of IBM and demanded that manager's

---

[31] Hamel, Gary; Valikangas, Lisa, *The Quest for Resilience*; Boston, MA, Harvard Business Review, September 2003.

work together to re-establish IBM's mission as a customer-focused provider of computing solutions, rather than a confederation of autonomous business units.[32]

Figure 4.4 Business Model Level

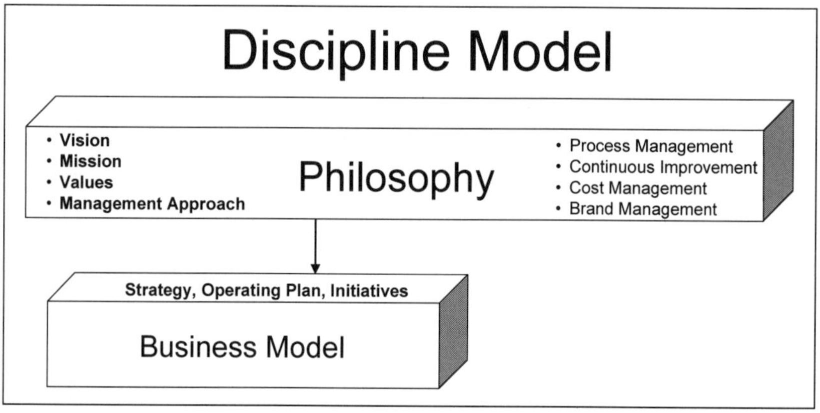

Discipline Model

- Vision
- Mission
- Values
- Management Approach

Philosophy

- Process Management
- Continuous Improvement
- Cost Management
- Brand Management

Strategy, Operating Plan, Initiatives

Business Model

"Strategy is the framework of choices that determine the nature and direction of an organization. A strategy positions a business – be it a company, division, agency, region, or department – in its external environment..."[33] The strategy captured in the business model takes a long-term perspective, evolving to support the vision. The strategic approach taken by the organization is strongly influenced by the philosophy. If this linkage is not recognized and established, it will be difficult for an organization to

---

[32] Gerstner, Louis V., *Who Says the Elephants Can't Dance? Inside IBM's Historic Turnaround*, New York, NY: HarperCollins Publishing 2002.
[33] Brache, Alan P., *How Organizations Work: Taking a Holistic Approach to Enterprise Health*, New York, NY: John Wiley and Sons, 2002, p.51.

successfully implement its strategy- the strategy is working against how the organization operates.

With the strategy established, the operating plan and resulting initiatives are periodically updated based on current conditions. As an example, if an organization has a strategy targeting entry into a new market, an initiative supporting that could be to gain 10% market share in the current year by cross-selling the new product into the existing customer base.

Most organizations update the strategy and operating plan annually, and link it to the budgeting cycle. Some organizations have started to update the operating plan and budget on a more frequent basis, recognizing that business conditions change quickly, and require a shorter planning cycle. Whichever approach is used, initiatives get added as the business needs warrant. The filter for adding initiatives should be the strategy of the organization. All organizations are resource constrained, so it is critical that initiatives support the direction established in the strategy.

The business model changes and evolves as markets and customer conditions warrant. This evolution can be gradual, with periodic disruptive technologies (the Internet) or events (September 11, 2001) causing more radical changes to the model. But the philosophy is the bedrock; it remains the anchor to which the business model is tied.

As organizations implement initiatives to support the strategy, they should consider proven and well-developed methodologies and tools that have been formulated over time. The selection of the correct methods and tools is the key to the success of any initiative.

4.4 METHODS

The layer supporting the business model includes the methods used in the organization to execute the strategy and support the direction provided by the philosophy. These methods could be viewed as laying out the steps required to implement initiatives (using a construction example, "how to nail"). These methods are recognized methodologies that have well-developed and time-tested steps. They are well-recognized approaches. Numerous articles and books have been written that teach organizations how to apply these methods. The appropriate methods support the strategic objectives of the organization and are required to implement the initiatives identified in the operating plan.

Examples of methods that may be used in an organization include:

- CAM-I ABC/M Model©
- Capability Maturity Model (CMM)
- Baldrige Award criteria
- Balanced Scorecard®
- Quality standards (such as ISO, QFD, QS, and TQL)
- Economic Value Added

- Six Sigma
- Continuous improvement
- Project Management
- Change Management
- Process-Based Accounting[34]

Note that Continuous Improvement can be included in both the Philosophy and Method levels. The importance and emphasis in the organization will determine at what level it will reside.

How a methodology is selected is critical to its longevity and usefulness. Consider two different approaches. In the first approach, the organization updates the operating plan (that supports a well thought out strategy), and identifies initiatives needed to accomplish the identified objectives. A methodology is then chosen that can be used to undertake and complete the initiative.

Or the organization may rely on a second approach. A manager returns from a conference after hearing an intriguing presentation describing a new methodology and the steps that were taken to implement "XYZ" at a company he admires. The manager has never heard of the methodology before, but "if it worked for them, it should help us." The next day, he calls his team and kicks off a project to install the "XYZ" methodology in his organization.

---

[34] Brimson, James, *Handbook of Process-Based Accounting: Leveraging Processes to Predict Results*, New York, NY: AICPA, 2002.

Figure 4.5 Methods Level

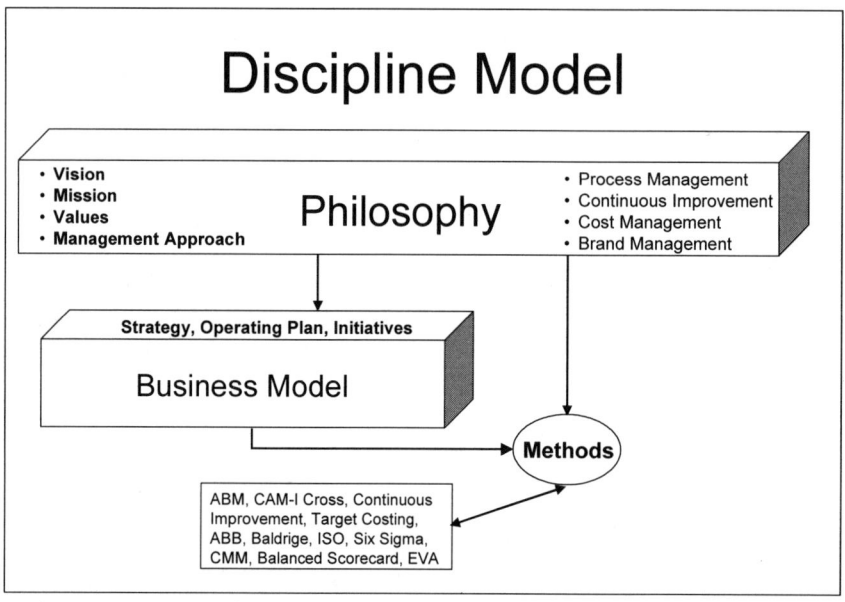

Which approach has the greatest chance of success? In the first instance, the methodology chosen was to complete an initiative supporting the strategy. In the second instance, the next "flavor of the month" project has begun. A method has been brought in because it helped someone else, with no consideration of how it fits to the strategy, and philosophy, of the organization. Alan Brache has also described this situation as, "Improvement 'medication' frequently taken without diagnosis. No organizational equivalent of a comprehensive physical exam."[35] Pity the employees who suffer at the whim of a management team that lacks the

---

[35] Brache, Alan P.,"Covering the Waterfront of Change: The Nine Variables that Influence Organizational Performance" *CAM-I Quarterly Research Conference Presentation*, June 10, 2003, San Diego, CA.

discipline to put methodologies in the context of the strategy and overall philosophy.

Figure 4.6 shows the two approaches to introducing methods into an organization. These can be summarized as an aligned approach versus a random approach. The random approach most often would take less time, but usually results in failure. It was never identified how the method fit into the organization or addressed the objectives identified in the strategy. The aligned approach takes more time to get it right, but significantly increases the methods chances for long-term success, which is judged by value added to the organization.

After a method has been in place for an extended period, and has provided value to the organization, the method begins to become part of the management approach embedded in the organization's mindset. **A method's effectiveness and longevity is significantly influenced by how well it is aligned to the philosophy and the strategy in the business model**. Where alignment exists, management is using the data and information generated by the method to monitor and improve the business. The ongoing dialogue around which decisions are made requires that the method's output support the business model. Executives and managers use the method to make decisions.

Figure 4.6 Discipline Model Contrasted with Ad hoc Model

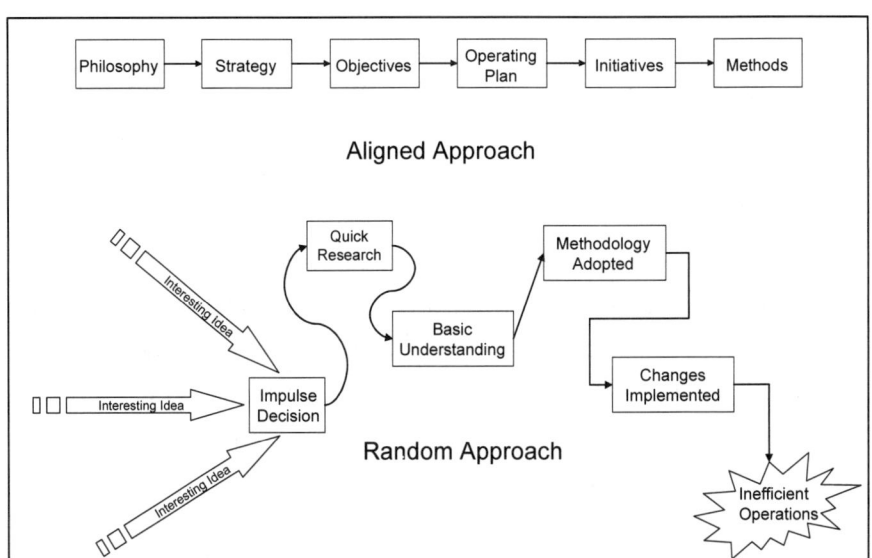

Where no such alignment exists, managers and executives often do not use the output generated by the method. Sooner or later, the method fades away; the sponsor gives up and moves on.

This can be seen very clearly with methods such as the Balanced Scorecard and ABM. In one organization, the Balanced Scorecard was brought in by a planning manager who knew the impact it could have communicating strategy and aligning performance. A broader group of managers were engaged in the concept and developed the scorecard, seeing the impact that a clear sense of direction can provide. But when it was presented to the senior executives, it was rejected. Senior management had no desire to be aligned. They did not have a clear strategy or well-defined business model (that is a prime responsibility of the senior management team). A vision for the organization had not been clearly articulated or even developed. The management model was in flux as the executives tried to determine or change their management approach. In this organization, the guiding principles and focus (the philosophy) had not been clearly established and defined. As a result, this method languished and then died. As could be expected, that organization continues to struggle. In examples like this, methods have little chance to be effective, and will not have a long tenure.

4.5 TOOLS

At the bottom layer of the Discipline Model are the tools that support the methods. These are the specific devices used (the "hammer"). The tools are required for the methods to be successful. **Tools are the enablers, not the drivers, of change**.

Examples of tools that support methods used with a Process Based Management approach include:

- ABC (cost drivers, activity dictionary)
- Process maps (relationship maps, flow charts)
- Six Sigma tools (such as Statistical Process Control)
- Project Management tools (such as MS Project)

- Quality control tools (such as control charts, cause and effect diagram, Pareto diagrams, and Quality Functional Deployment)
- ERP (Enterprise Resource Planning)

These tools are required to make the methods they support successful. If an organization is using the Six Sigma method to improve the organization, it needs specific Six Sigma tools to be successful. Use of the tools without the overall methodology will also not lead to success.

Figure 4.7 Tools Level

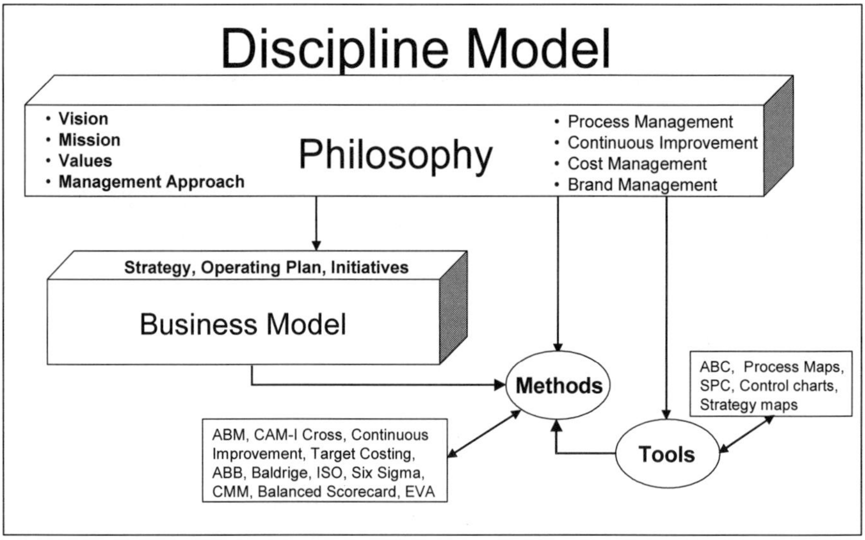

Discipline Model

- Vision
- Mission
- Values
- Management Approach

Philosophy

- Process Management
- Continuous Improvement
- Cost Management
- Brand Management

Strategy, Operating Plan, Initiatives

Business Model

ABM, CAM-I Cross, Continuous Improvement, Target Costing, ABB, Baldrige, ISO, Six Sigma, CMM, Balanced Scorecard, EVA

Methods

ABC, Process Maps, SPC, Control charts, Strategy maps

Tools

Tools are often randomly introduced into organizations (the same challenge that was discussed with methods). Someone from a department goes to a conference and is introduced to a new tool that "everyone" should be using. It may or may not get traction; if it does, it now begins to compete with all the tools that are being tried. All tool initiators are looking for a higher-level sponsor, someone who can raise the visibility of this new tool and tie it to another method or initiative underway in the organization. These tools often fail to get traction, are not aligned with any method or the overriding philosophy, and consequently fade away.

The key to effective implementation of a tool is to support a method in place in the organization. A tool must be looked at in the context of the entire organization. Without this linkage, a tool cannot be aligned to the business model and philosophy. Lacking this alignment, the tool is destined for the closet with all the other tools that once made sense to someone, but proved inappropriate for the organization.

Examples of tools that fall into this category are abundant. The problem is not the tool; it is the decision to implement the tool without the right alignment. Two recent examples, ERP and CRM, point out the expensive pitfalls of tools. An organization should only implement an ERP or CRM package (a tool) if:

- The long-term strategy requires it
- A methodology is in place (such as project management and continuous improvement) to support it.

- It is in sync with the organizational philosophy, including its mission, vision and values.
- The underlying processes have been defined.

If you successfully implement a tool but the tool does not provide any value to the organization, the tool should never have been introduced in the first place. If an organization follows the concepts outlined in the Discipline Model, this is less likely to occur.

4.6 WHY IS THE DISCIPLINE MODEL IMPORTANT?

With so many different methods and tools being introduced and brought into organizations, it is no wonder that most are not successful. They all work to some degree and provide benefits to organizations. However, customer value comes from alignment with the philosophy and the business model.

An organization needs a defined philosophy and a supporting business model to be able to identify what methods and tools will help move the organization forward to reach its vision and goals. A tool will not have a long life if it is not tied to a method that supports the business model and the philosophy. A method not anchored in the business model and the philosophy will fade away. It is not a matter of "IF" it will fade away; it is a matter of "WHEN". This model provides a discipline that organizations can follow to successfully implement methods and tools that are "right" for their organizations.

With a philosophy and business model firmly established, there is now a way to select and prioritize methods and tools. In "Spotting Management Fads," Miller and Hartwick[36] discuss how to tell a fad from a tool that might endure. However, that is only part of the issue. The key is aligning the tools to methods, and methods to a business model, and to an enduring management philosophy in the organization.

It is our observation that Process Based Management should be a key component of the philosophy for many organizations. What is interesting is that organizations like Southwest Airlines have attained success partly as a result of this holistic, process-based focus, but do not use the term Process Based Management. It has become part of their core way of life and has been ingrained into the philosophy and the mindset of the organization.

Other organizations are in the early stages in their journey to becoming process based. The Discipline Model provides a framework to identify the different initiatives, methods and tools already in place that can be linked into the process efforts. It is important to recognize the various initiatives that serve as entry points into Process Based Management and to leverage those entry points to develop a

---

[36] Miller, Danny and Jon Hartwick, "Spotting Management Fads," *Harvard Business Review*, October 2002, p. 26-27.

focused approach. The model provides a framework to guide those discussions and to develop an appropriate approach given the current business model and philosophy.

4.7 APPLYING THE DISCIPLINE MODEL

The Discipline Model can be applied in an organization to identify how methods and tools can support your business model and philosophy.

The organization needs to follow some fundamental steps:

- Identify the overall philosophy of the organization. Review the strategy and identify how it flows from and supports the philosophy.
- Review the operating plan. Identify and list all the initiatives that are active in the organization and detail the history of each (such as how it was introduced, when, and groups involved). An example of a chart showing a timeline for initiatives is shown at Figure 4.8. Identify the link of each initiative to the operating plan and the strategy.
- Identify the methods and tools in use and how they support either an initiative or are part of the management approach. Where the methods or tools are not linked, trace the history to determine how they came into use in the organization.

Figure 4.8 Timeline for Initiatives

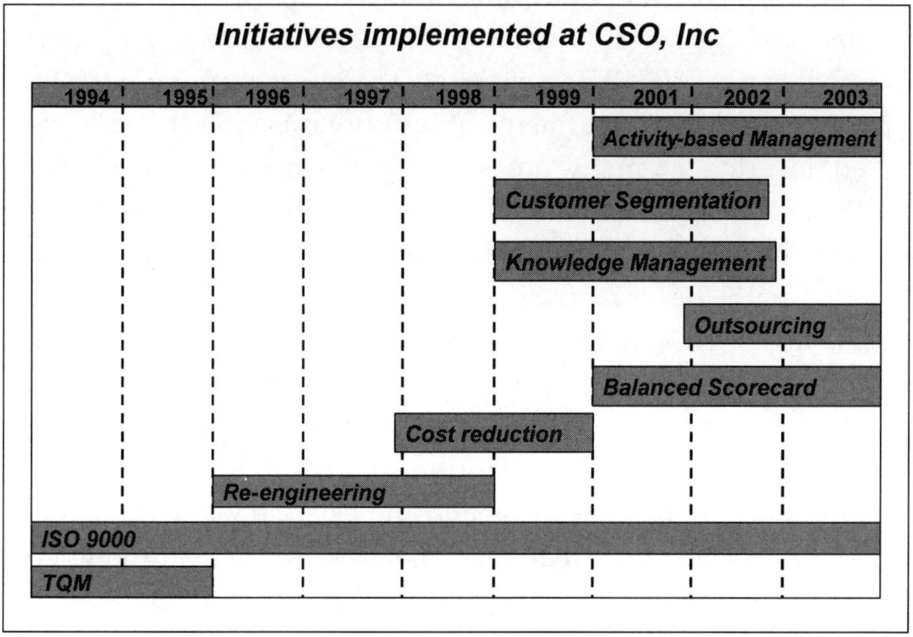

Initiatives implemented at CSO, Inc

1994	1995	1996	1997	1998	1999	2001	2002	2003

Activity-based Management

Customer Segmentation

Knowledge Management

Outsourcing

Balanced Scorecard

Cost reduction

Re-engineering

ISO 9000

TQM

- Identify methods and tools needed in the organization that are not in place.

When the organization has followed these steps, it will have a solid understanding of all the initiatives, methods, and tools that are in place, and how they link to what the organization is trying to accomplish. They will also know what is not linked (and should be eliminated), as well as where there is a need for a methodology to support the direction in the business model. It will have a profile of the initiatives in the organization.

As organizations mature in their use of Process Based Management, the Discipline model helps filter initiatives. Just as important as what methods and tools are used is what is not used. As an example, there was a strong push by the planning department of an organization to use re-engineering in many areas of the business. However, the Process Council (which oversees the overall process effort and the process teams) concluded that method was not in sync with the organization's values and the Process Based Management approach that promoted continuous improvement. Other methods and tools get evaluated in a similar manner. As employees attend seminars and read trade publications, they can filter out what would not work based on the process focus and the clear strategic direction. Methods and tools that may make sense, and are aligned with the business model, are introduced in pilot projects to see if they add value. If they pass the value test, they would then become part of an operating plan initiative identified as part of the strategic plan. The widespread understanding of the strategy and the organization's processes eliminates much wasted effort and resource constraints when methods and tools do not make sense.

THE NEXT STEPS

The Discipline Model is used in conjunction with the Process Based Management Assessment Framework, which is addressed in the next chapter. The Assessment Framework is used to determine how well an organization is implementing Process Based Management. The Assessment

Framework measures how mature the organization has become on its journey to becoming a process-based organization. The Discipline Model provides a profile of the various methods and tools in use in the organization, and how they are aligned to the business model and the philosophy. That understanding is essential to understanding and completing the assessment of any organization.

CHAPTER 5:

ASSESSMENT FRAMEWORK AND CASE STUDY FINDINGS

OBJECTIVES:

1) Describe the Process Based Management Assessment Model and Assessment Framework.

2) Present the case study findings, insights and conclusions

The first section of the book provided the groundwork for the management approach we call Process Based Management. The benefits of this management approach were outlined to explain how it is different than traditional functional management.

The Discipline model was introduced in Chapter 4 as the first model in the Process Based Management Loop (Figure 5.1). This model shows how any organization can identify the linkage between all the various initiatives underway. It is important to make that linkage because it provides a profile of the initiatives, which is used to determine the direction of the organization. With that profile, we have a starting point to assess how an organization is progressing in implementing Process Based Management. This leads to the Process Based Management Assessment Model, which is the basis of performing organizational assessments.

Figure 5.1 Process Based Management Loop

Process Based Management Loop

Discipline Model

Implementation Action Plan

Profile

Process Continuum Model

Process Based Management Assessment Model

Maturity Level

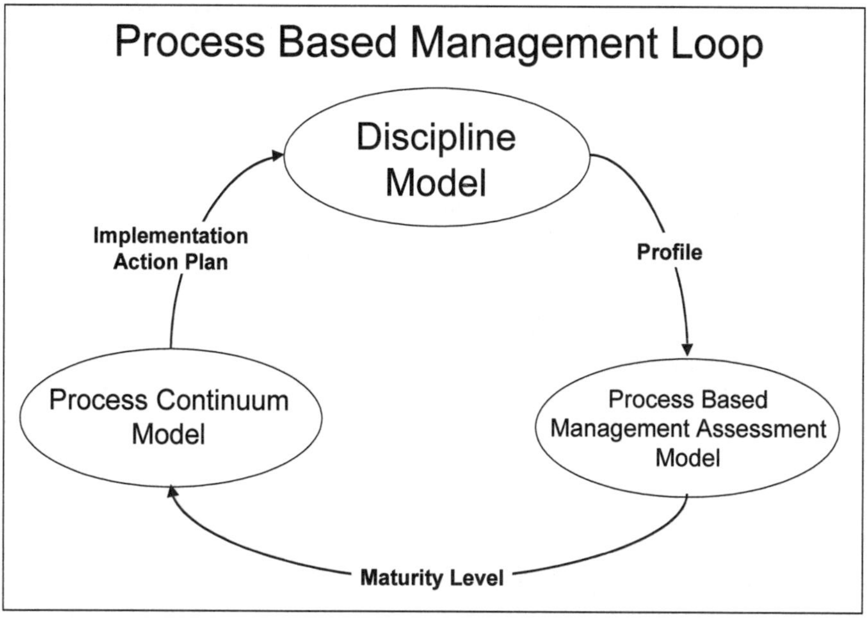

5.1 ASSESSMENT BACKGROUND

In 1994 a group of organizations came together in CAM-I to form a process management research group to inform and educate organizations about process based management.

The initial companies were:

- Texas Instruments
- IBM
- Valmet (now named Metso Corporation - Finland)
- Chrysler (now part of Daimler-Chrysler)
- Allied Signal (now part of Honeywell)
- GTE (now part of Verizon)

These companies wanted to understand the critical success factors for migrating to a process-centered approach for organizing and managing their activities. They all had tried reengineering and had seen the problems and challenges that it creates; but they also perceived the benefits of a processed-based approach. They also wanted to understand how they could integrate the multiple initiatives that were the reality in each of their organizations. There had to be a better way.

The first Phase ran from 1994 to 1997. It focused on capturing the process knowledge of these six organizations, each of which was trying to determine what it could do differently to achieve their process objectives. These organizations had some tough challenges that are very common to many organizations:

- They were heavily involved in process reengineering
- Reengineering had reduced costs but negatively impacted customer satisfaction

- They realized that a process approach was the key to lasting benefits.

The result of that three year project was captured in "The Road to Excellence: Becoming a Process-Based Company" (published in 1997[37]). The book provides a framework that focuses on the fundamental "shifts" required for a typical functionally oriented organization to move to a process orientation. The premise is straightforward: *An organization is only as effective as its processes.* Organizations need to focus on how things happen and how they can happen better, as well as understand how resources are consumed across functional and departmental boundaries. In order to make this "shift", managers must examine their mindset, their measures, their methods and the interaction among these elements.

The Process Management Framework introduced in the Road to Excellence consisted of five sections:

- Mindset Shift
    - Creating the Vision (and Strategy)
    - Process Clarity
    - Process Awareness
    - Process Ownership and Control
- Migration to a Process-Centered Organization
- Process Analysis

---

[37] Daly, Dennis C. Daly and Tom Freeman, *The Road to Excellence: Becoming a Process-based Company*, Bedford, TX: Consortium for Advanced Manufacturing-International, 1997.

- Process-Based Performance Measures
- Continuous Process Management

Once this framework was established, another group of companies with similar issues wanted to apply the process framework to their organizations. These organizations realized that they needed to extend the work of the original research to:

- *Validate* and *expand* the framework based on the experience of other organizations
- **Research** and **document** other key learning's and critical success factors

5.2 CASE STUDY APPROACH

A case study approach was chosen as the mechanism to validate the framework and extend the knowledge of the group. The goal of the case study approach is to assess and document the experiences of different types of organizations. The research group wanted to understand the different approaches that organizations had taken to becoming process-based as well as the progress they had achieved.

The validation process required:

- A visual of the framework (Figure 5.2)
- An assessment instrument based on the framework

A set of questions was developed for each of the main categories in the framework. The questions established common criteria that were used to validate the framework and compare each of the organizations.

The CAM-I Process Management Interest Group developed the assessment questions over the course of one year. During that time they examined *The Road to Excellence* framework in great depth, studied process-related case studies from North America and Scandinavia, and reviewed past assessments and experiences drawn from consulting engagements. The result was the assessment questions to conduct the case studies.

5.3 THE PROCESS BASED MANAGEMENT ASSESSMENT FRAMEWORK

A visual depiction of the Assessment Framework and the assessment criteria was developed to communicate the areas of Process Based Management addressed during the assessment process. The categories in the Road to Excellence were carried forward into Figure 5.2; the Process Analysis section is included in Continuous improvement. This visual evolved to identify the areas where an organization should focus its efforts as they move along the journey to Process Based Management.

Figure 5.2 Process Based Management Assessment
Framework

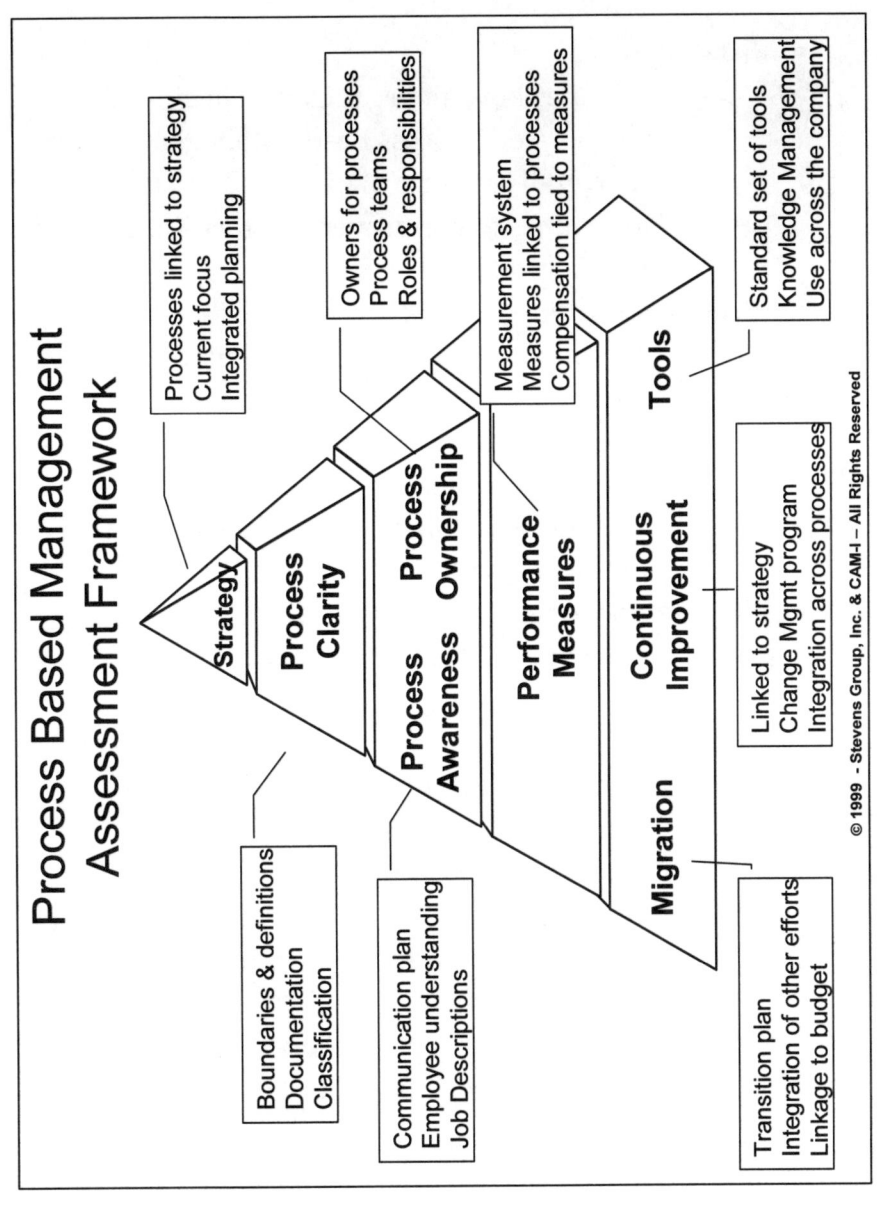

© 1999 - Stevens Group, Inc. & CAM-I – All Rights Reserved

The assessment framework criteria consist of the following sections:

- **Strategy**
    - Examines how an organization has incorporated Process Based Management into the overall strategic plan
    - Determines the improvement focus of an organization
- **Process Clarity**
    - Determines if processes have defined boundaries
    - Identifies what documentation exists for defined processes
    - Identifies what process classification framework is used
- **Process Awareness**
    - Determines if a communication plan exists for ongoing process awareness
    - Examines how well employees understand their role in process execution
    - Determines if job descriptions have been defined in terms of process
- **Process Ownership**
    - Determines if process owners are in place and their effectiveness,
    - Examines what type of process teams exist along with associated training

- Determines how well roles and responsibilities are defined for process owners, teams and leaders
- **Performance Measures**
  - Examines what type of measurement system is used to gauge process performance
  - Identifies how process performance is linked to compensation
- **Migration**
  - Determines if the organization has developed a plan for transitioning to Process Based Management
  - Examines how other initiatives are linked into an overall process strategy.
  - Assesses how the organization is migrating to process-based budgets
- **Continuous Improvement**
  - Determines if improvement opportunities are linked to strategy
  - Examines how the strategy drives improvement efforts
  - Examines what type of change management program is in place for process changes
  - Determines how integration occurs across processes
- **Tools**
  - Determines what types of tools are used for Process Based Management
  - Examines how tools are integrated across multiple initiatives

As the research has continued and the knowledge base has expanded, it has become evident that an assessment is an essential initial step for an organization pursuing a process-based approach. The assessment provides a baseline for determining gaps, identifying areas to focus on and prioritizing next steps.

5.4 HOW IS THIS ASSESSMENT DIFFERENT?

There are other types of assessments that exist in the marketplace today, such as Baldrige Award for Performance Excellence, Software Engineering Institute's (SEI) Capability Maturity Model (CMM) and Supply-Chain Council's Award for Supply Chain Excellence. These assessments evaluate organizational performance, process and project management maturity, or project execution for a supply chain.

The Process Based Management assessment is targeted at determining how an organization is changing its "management approach" to become process-based, rather than targeting the specific performance of individual processes. The key difference is that embedding process thinking in the management approach provides an increased chance of long-term success.

5.5 CASE STUDY FINDINGS

The observations from the case studies and related research led the group to identify specific conclusions for each of the following four sections:

- *Mindset Shift* (which includes strategy, process clarity, and process awareness) - addresses the key component of cultural change that is often a gap in most business process improvement and reengineering initiatives.
- *Process-Based Measures* - examines the measurement system organizations utilize to measure process performance and how measures tie to individual incentives.
- *Migration* - determines if an organization has developed a transition plan for migrating to Process Based Management and how other types of initiatives (such as ABM, ISO, Six Sigma, and Lean) have been integrated into transition plans.
- *Continuous Process Management* - evaluates an organization's overall progress towards embedding Process Based Management.

Each section is divided into the following:

- A description of the key items examined in the assessment
- An analysis of the observations for each category

- How each case study company scored in the assessment categories

A scoring scale was developed to indicate how the organization had progressed:

0-19 – No approach, ad hoc
20-39 – Reactive approach
40-59 – Beginning of systematic approach
60-79 – Stable, systematic approach
80-100 – Proactive approach

5.5.1 MINDSET SHIFT

The objective of this section is to address the changes required in both management and individual behaviors that affect the mindset of an organization. The section focuses on determining how well organizations have aligned their strategy and initiatives to sustain long-term cultural change. Most organizations are successful at implementing a new program or initiative in the short term, but few are able to maintain the discipline to change the underlying philosophy.

A second focus examines how well processes have been defined and communicated throughout the organization, along with the structure (in terms of process owners, process leaders and process teams) for managing ongoing processes.

The Mindset Shift section is divided into the following four categories:

- *Strategy*
- *Process Clarity*
- *Process Awareness*
- *Process Ownership*

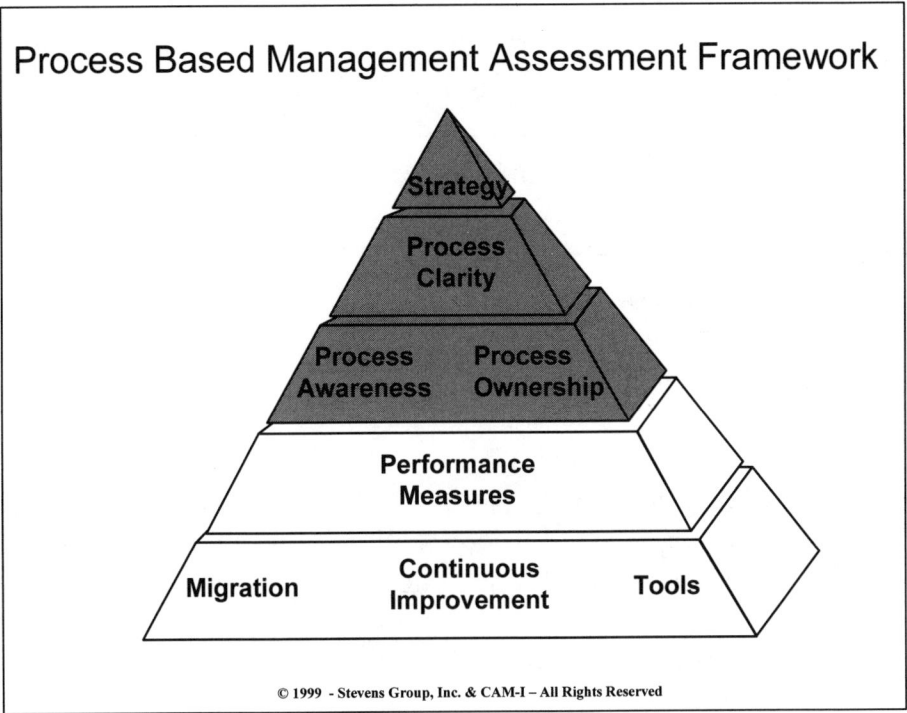

Process Based Management Assessment Framework

© 1999 - Stevens Group, Inc. & CAM-I – All Rights Reserved

5.5.1.1 STRATEGY

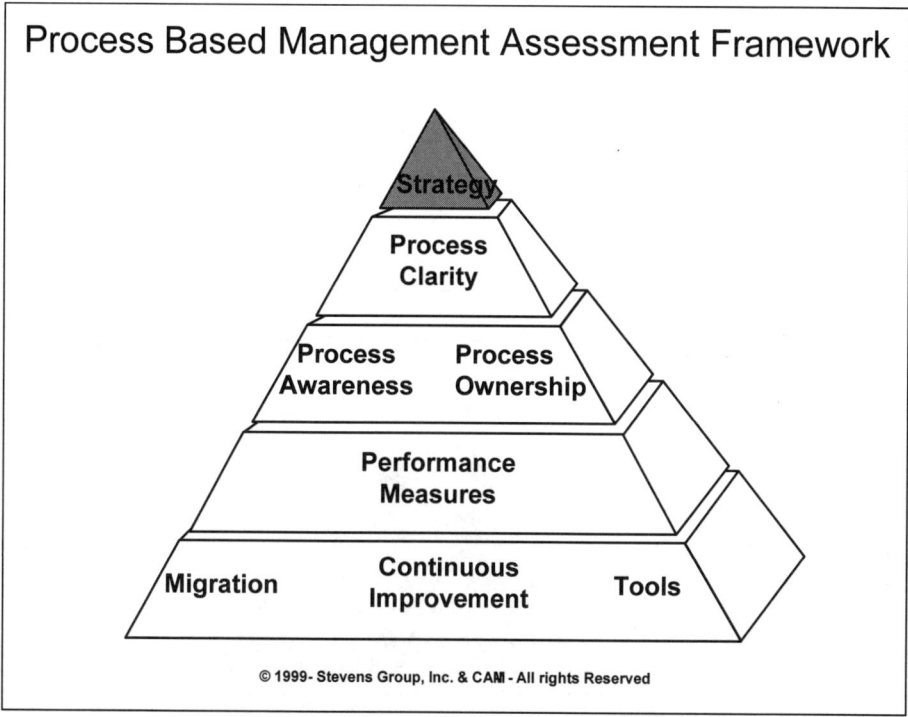

Process Based Management Assessment Framework

Strategy

Process Clarity

Process Awareness   Process Ownership

Performance Measures

Migration   Continuous Improvement   Tools

© 1999- Stevens Group, Inc. & CAM - All rights Reserved

Strategy has a significant impact on driving cultural change and is a key in determining how an organization embeds Process Based Management.

STRATEGY KEY ITEMS

- Unlike other types of assessments that look at whether a strategic plan exists, this assessment examines what management approach drives the current strategy of the organization, and whether Process Based Management is part of the overall strategy.

- Communication of a process-based strategy to all stakeholders is examined along with the feedback mechanisms for customers, process owners, employees and other stakeholders to provide input into an integrated planning process.

- The existence of a process vision and how the strategic plan links core competencies to key processes is examined.

- The evaluation of operating plans and initiatives defined in the strategic plan is a critical aspect of determining if an organization is fully committed to a process-based strategy. The initiatives and action plans need to address incentives, training and organizational alignment, along with specific goals and objectives for measuring the performance of key processes.

STRATEGY CASE STUDY OBSERVATIONS

Strategy is one of the *least* addressed factors in the implementation of Process Based Management. The case studies revealed the following key observations and associated conclusions:

- Process Based Management was not present as part of the corporate strategy at most of the case study organizations. However, it was seen as part of departmental strategies.

Conclusion - The evolution to Process Based Management is still viewed as tactical, not strategic.

- When Process Based Management was part of the vision, mission, management approach, and strategy, and communicated throughout the organization, there was not a clear distinction between functional and process responsibilities. This illustrates that process-oriented thinking has not firmly taken root.

Conclusion – The Successful implementation of Process Based Management requires more that just stating that an organization will be process-based. It requires specific action plans to address incentives, training and organizational alignment.

- Starting with a strategy of business process redesign or a business process reengineering (BPR) initiative tends to focus the organization only on short-term gains without a full understanding of the long-term impact on customer service.

Conclusion – BPR alone is not an effective transition path for implementing Process Based Management as an overall strategy.

- Process Based Management, when applied to supply chain processes, provides the foundation for integrating strategies across multiple organizations, even when only one of the organizations is the primary driver.

Conclusion – Process Based Management is an effective strategy for integrating Supply Chains.

- Having specific plans and top-level management buy-in for implementing Process Based Management, without ownership and oversight for executing the plans, does not guarantee success.

Conclusion – Process Based Management needs to be viewed as an organizational strategy. As such, it requires executive oversight and ownership. It must focus on the continuous improvement of all processes and not be viewed as a project with a defined ending

STRATEGY SCORING SUMMARY

Figure 5.3 depicts the scores for the strategy category. The scores were all below the 60 percent range, which indicates that none of the case study organizations had a well-defined systematic approach for Process Based Management in their strategy. Two organizations did have Process Based Management as part of their corporate strategy with a well communicated plan and executive buy-in. However, neither organization successfully executed the plan.

Figure 5.3 Strategy

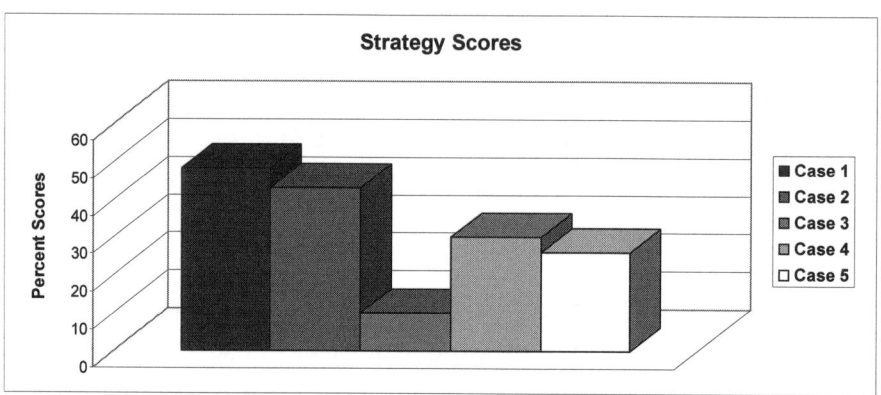

5.5.1.2 PROCESS CLARITY

Process Clarity focuses on how well processes have been defined, documented and communicated across the organization.

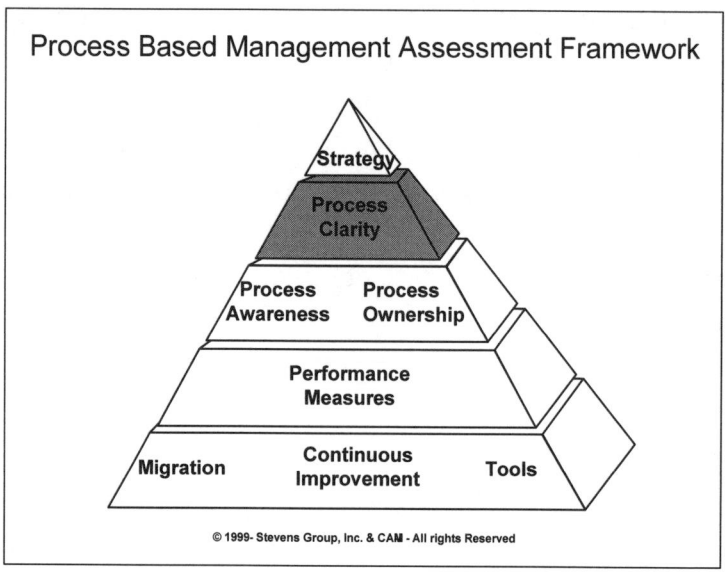

PROCESS CLARITY KEY ITEMS

- The assessment examines process boundaries and how they are defined and communicated.
- The use of a process classification structure to determine if the organization has developed a mechanism to prioritize processes.
- The definition of cross-functional boundaries, along with how agreement is reached on the boundaries of cross-functional processes.
- How customer requirements are captured and communicated to process owners and teams.

PROCESS CLARITY OBSERVATIONS

Process Clarity tended to be one of the strongest areas in many of the case organizations. The case studies revealed the following key observations and associated conclusions:

- The dedication of a group of employees responsible for developing, maintaining, and updating process documentation was seen in several organizations. These organizations tended to be more advanced in their approach to process clarity.

  Conclusion – Successful Process Clarity requires a dedicated staff to administer, facilitate, and promote processes.

- Many of the case-study organizations had detailed process maps and flowcharts depicting various levels of detail. However, some organizations had invested much time and effort in detailing "as is" processes at a "work instruction" level instead of focusing on process analysis to identify the sources of variability and the changes needed for improvement.

  Conclusion – Time has a greater return when spent on "to be" than on "as is" processes. Designing, improving, and deploying new processes is more productive than analyzing broken processes.

- A lack of consistency in the classification structure used for defining processes led to some processes mirroring the functional organization structure, with limited customer focus and interaction.

  Conclusion – Having a standard methodology for process classification ensures that processes are cross-functional and address the key interfaces with the customer.

- Even with detailed process documentation, dedicated staff to maintain process information, and a mechanism for updating processes, training and education were not linked to this process documentation.

  Conclusion – Process documentation is seen as a one-time event to support a specific project activity, not as a tool for training and educating employees on end-to-end processes.

- In case-study organizations where processes were clearly defined and documented, there was minimal knowledge of process requirements from external stakeholders and customers.

Conclusion – Process definition and design needs to include a mechanism to capture requirements from external stakeholders and customers.

PROCESS CLARITY SCORING SUMMARY

Figure 5.4 depicts varying levels of Process Clarity in the case study organizations. Several organizations scored in the higher range, having a well-defined systematic approach for Process Clarity, while others were in an ad-hoc mode. Organizations in the lower range tended to have an unclear definition of processes, using a functionally based or internal value chain classification.

Figure 5.4 Process Clarity

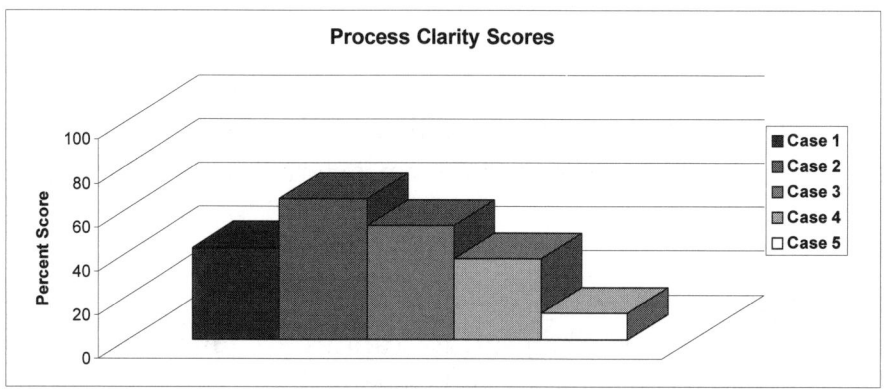

5.5.1.3 PROCESS AWARENESS

Process awareness is as important as strategy; however, it is typically viewed as a one-time event in the implementation plan, rather than an ongoing activity.

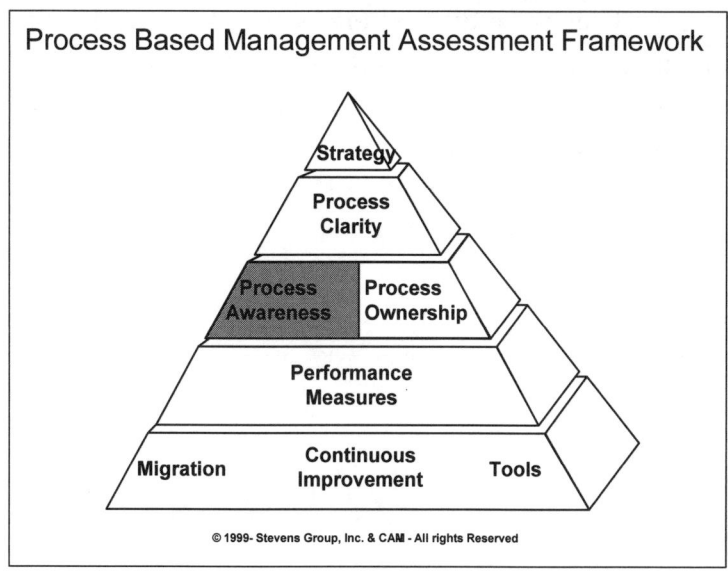

PROCESS AWARENESS KEY ITEMS

- The extent of clear roles and responsibilities for Process Based Management.
- Employee knowledge and understanding of key processes.
- To what extent employees describe their jobs in terms of key processes. In a process-based organization, employees tend to see their jobs as a part of a larger process, not as stand-alone functions.
- Customer knowledge and understanding of the organizations processes.

PROCESS AWARENESS OBSERVATIONS

A key factor evident in the majority of case organizations was that awareness was seen as a one-time event, not an ongoing communication program. The case studies revealed the following key observations and associated conclusions:

- Communication with employees is typically not done in terms of processes, thereby limiting an organization's effectiveness in transitioning to Process Based Management.

  Conclusion – Processes must continually be communicated and framed in a manner that employees can relate to. Employees need to understand their role in processes, and how ongoing actions in the company affect these processes.

- Employees who were engaged in process efforts were well-versed in process terminology and concepts; however, there were no ongoing plans for communication or training of individuals outside those efforts.

    Conclusion – An ongoing communication and training plan is critical in raising awareness of Process Based Management among all employees.

- An unclear process infrastructure (teams, owners, and performer roles and responsibilities) makes it diffcult to understand the difference between a process and a functional perspective.

    Conclusion – The Process Based Management infrastructure needs to be clearly defined and communicated throughout the organization. Every employee must understand their role in this infrastructure, and understand the responsibilities of each role in the infrsastructure.

- In most cases, job descriptions or job training did not acknowledge process responsibilities, making employee awareness of processes difficult.

Conclusion – An effective awareness program must address a change in job descriptions (such as adding process end-to-end responsibilities) and training to incorporate additional information regarding process focus.

- Where Process Awareness exists, it tends to be project oriented rather than process oriented, and communication is not made outside of the project team.

Conclusion – An ongoing communication plan is a key component for Process Based Management, and should address both process teams and all other employees.

PROCESS AWARENESS SCORING SUMMARY

Figure 5.5 depicts that Process Awareness is one of the lowest scoring categories in Mindset Shift, primarily because most organizations did not have a formal, ongoing communication plan. In some cases, the only communication that occurred was at the start of the project and typically involved only a few people affected by process changes. Most awareness programs tended to be ad hoc at best; only two organizations had any type of formal program in place.

A key point regarding awareness is that *You cannot over communicate!!*

Figure 5.5 Process Awareness

Process Awareness Scores
Percent Scores
100
80
60
40
20
0
Case 1
Case 2
Case 3
Case 4
Case 5

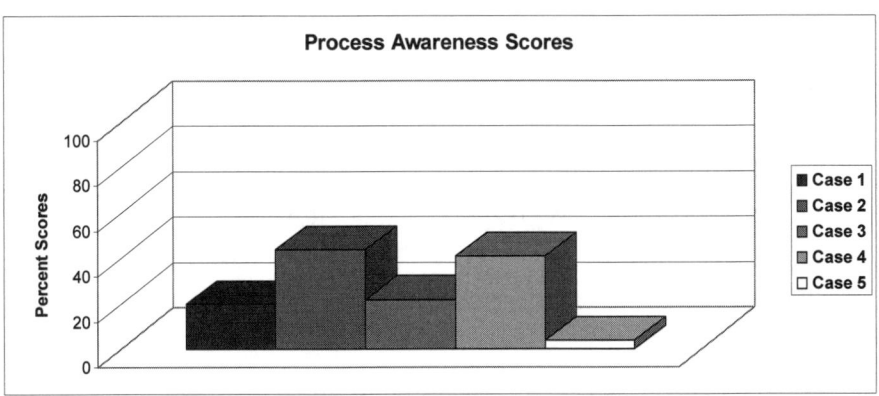

5.5.1.4 PROCESS OWNERSHIP

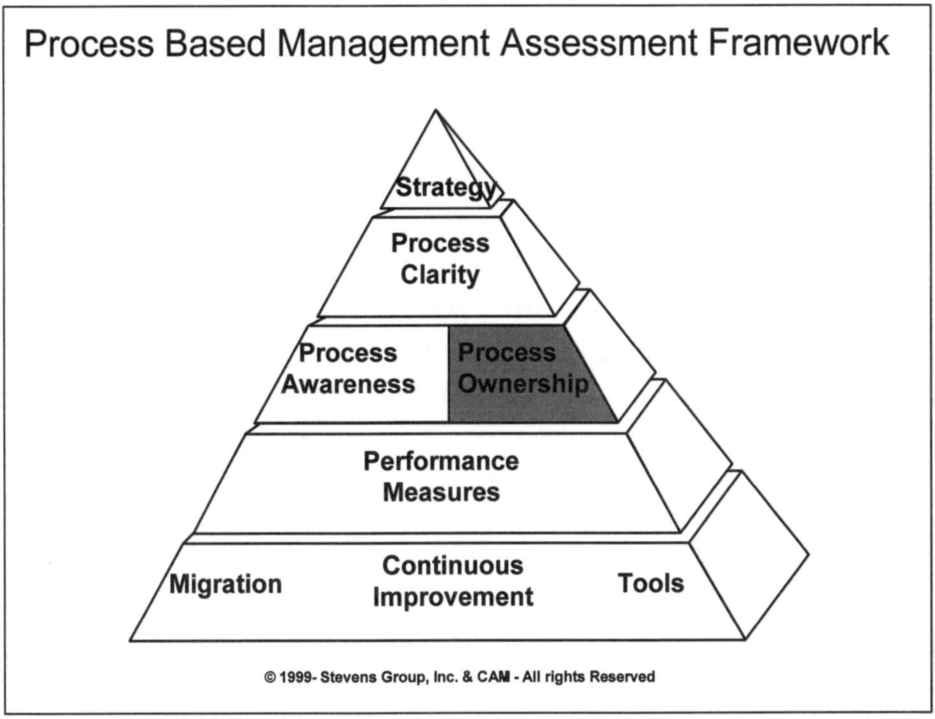

Process Based Management Assessment Framework
Strategy
Process Clarity
Process Awareness
Process Ownership
Performance Measures
Migration
Continuous Improvement
Tools
© 1999- Stevens Group, Inc. & CAM - All rights Reserved

Ownership addresses the critical aspects of process owners, process teams, and the overall Process Based Management infrastructure.

PROCESS OWNERSHIP KEY ITEMS

- The assessment determines whether process owners exist, their responsibilities and level in the organization, and the interaction among process owners.

- Also examined are how process owners are held accountable and how ownership differences are resolved between functional and process priorities.

- Training for process owners and teams is evaluated along with the criteria used to select both owners and team members.

PROCESS OWNERSHIP OBSERVATIONS

Two common observations in the case study organizations were:

(1) the lack of process owners overall; and
(2) when owners did exist, they were at the wrong level in the organization.

The case studies revealed the following key observations and associated conclusions:

- Process owners have all of the accountability for a process but none of the authority. Process owners do not have the authority to make end-to-end changes.

  Conclusion – Process owners must be at the executive level so that they can drive behavior and influence decision-making.

- Process governance was not in place. The opportunity to speak with the same voice and give the process owners a chance to talk with one another was missing. There was no established forum for discussion (such as a process owner council) with the authority needed to define priorities and resolve issues.

  Conclusion – A formal process governance structure is a critical success factor to set priorities, resolve cross process issues, and manage resources.

- A formal training program for process owners, teams, and performers was not evident at most of the case study companies. Only one case study company committed the resources to develop:

  - An in-depth process management training program for those having significant leadership responsibility.
  - An introductory training program and a "train the trainer" program to expand process management training throughout the organization.

- A formal education process to familiarize all personnel with the purpose and processes of the organization.

Conclusion – A formal training program for process owners, process teams, and process performers is essential for successful implementation of Process Based Management.

- The naming of executive-level process owners does not ensure that process ownership is clearly understood, as made evident by the comment "I don't know what I do differently when I have my Process Owner hat on versus my functional hat."

Conclusion – Clearly defined roles and responsibilities for process owners and teams are critical to delineate between functional versus process responsibilities.

- "Process owner" is not a recognized term. Since most of the core processes corresponded primarily to an organizational department or division, ownership was seen as the responsibility of functional vice-president and manager levels.

Conclusion – Without formal recognition of the role of Process Owner, any attempt to implement Process Based Management will be unsuccessful.

- Process teams were established to design new processes; however, they were not involved in implementation or ongoing monitoring of process performance.

  Conclusion – Process teams must be seen as "permanent" in nature with periodic rotation of members.

PROCESS OWNERSHIP SCORING SUMMARY

Figure 5.6 reveals one of the key disconnects found in most of the case study organizations: Process Ownership is not understood as a critical component in implementing Process Based Management.   Most organizations were reactive, at best, when it came to having a management structure to support process owners and teams.   Those organizations that had a structure were missing the underlying training, and defined roles and responsibilities for successful Process Ownership.

Figure 5.6 Process Ownership

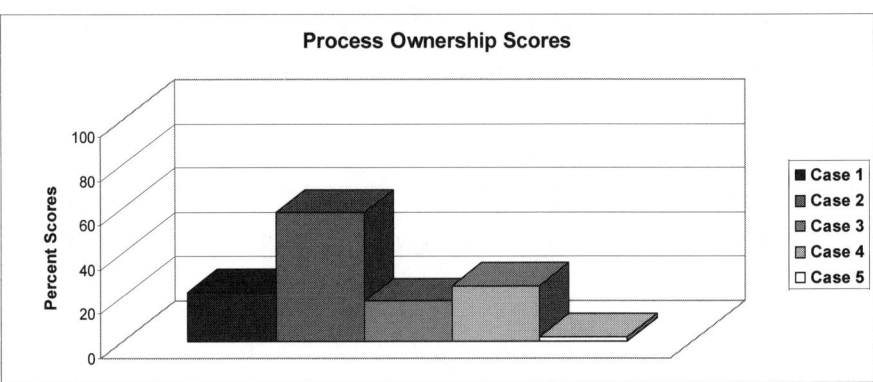

SCORING SUMMARY – MINDSET SHIFT

Overall, only one case study organization demonstrated the beginnings of a systematic approach to changing the mindset in their organization. The rest had pieces in place but no consistent approach.

Figure 5.7 Overall Mindset Shift Scoring

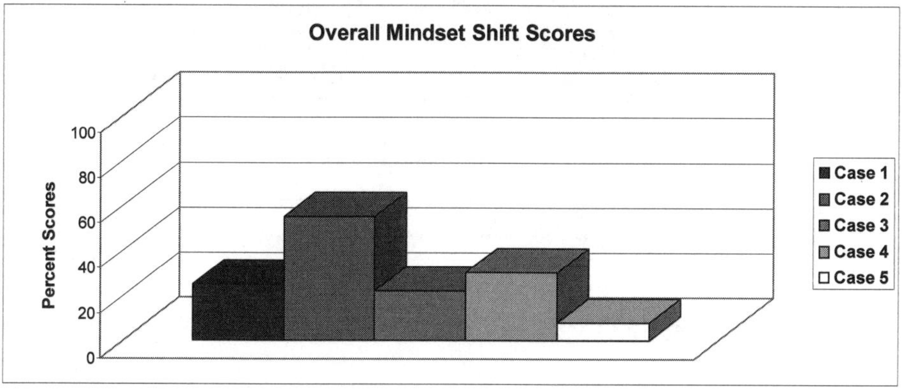

Overall Mindset Shift Scores

PROCESS-BASED PERFORMANCE MEASURES SECTION

5.5.2 PROCESS-BASED PERFORMANCE MEASURES

The Performance Measures category reviews three aspects of performance to determine if an organization has performance criteria and measures that are based on process performance.

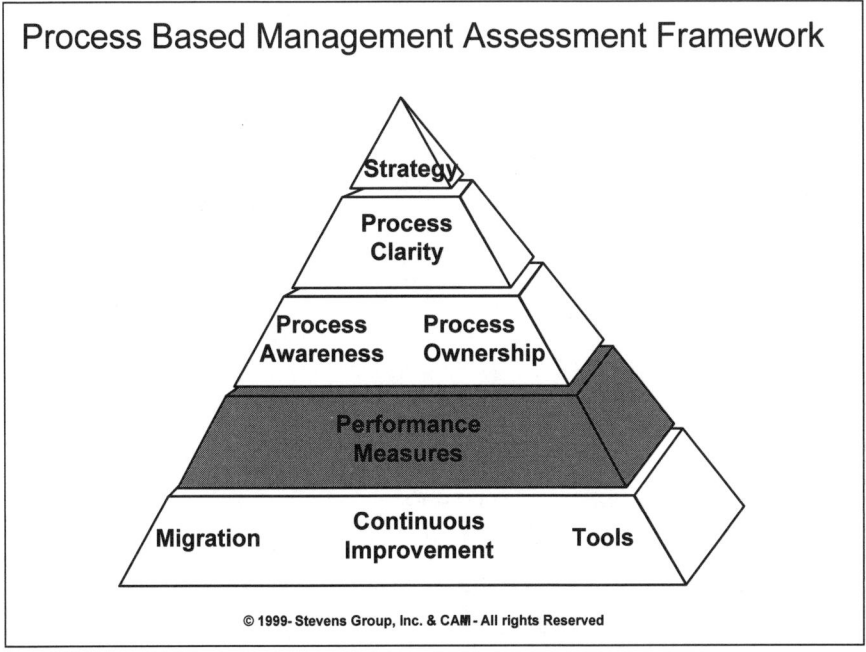

Process Based Management Assessment Framework

© 1999- Stevens Group, Inc. & CAM - All rights Reserved

PROCESS-BASED PERFORMANCE MEASURES KEY ITEMS

- *Measurement System* - Determines the type of measures that exist and whether they are functional or process-based. The assessment also reviews how process-based measures were developed and how the organization transitioned their measurement system.

- *Alignment* – Examines if measures are aligned with process goals and objectives, along with the linkage of process performance measures to strategic plans.

- *Compensation/Incentives* - Evaluates the tie between compensation and incentives for process performers, and process performance objectives. The tie to compensation and incentives also includes how process owners are evaluated and measured based on overall process performance.

PROCESS-BASED PERFORMANCE MEASURES CASE STUDY OBSERVATIONS

Of all the sections, Performance Measures is probably the one that is the most challenging and takes the longest to implement, particularly the compensation and incentives aspect. The case studies revealed the following key observations and associated conclusions:

- A measurement system with a market focus and process-driven structure was developed based on "white space" measurements. However, there was limited distribution of process measures to process owners and performers (less than 20 people knew the existence of the measurement maps). As good as the process measure maps are, they will not drive behavior unless they are widely distributed and understood.

  Conclusion – For process-based measures to be effective, they must be well communicated and linked with the deployment of new process designs.

- Process performance measures were more developed than the understanding and development of the process being measured. Extensive effort was invested in developing performance measures, while minimal work was done on developing the associated process details. This led to a disconnect between the measures and the processes being deployed.

Conclusion – A balance between the level of detail of process designs and performance measures must exist for them to be deployed and managed successfully.

- A strategic plan was developed that addressed incentive plans and the evaluation of process performance; however, it progressed no further and was never implemented. Performance measures were still viewed as individual report cards, not as process improvement tools.

Conclusion – Process performance measures and individual compensation and incentives must be linked for measures to be an effective tool in changing the mindset of the organization.

- Process measures were identified and defined by process teams; however, there was no owner assigned to monitor and report the results of the measures, thus leading to ineffective measurement of the "health" of the process.

Conclusion – Process measures require an owner to monitor and assess the effectiveness of the process and make modifications based on performance trends.

- Key performance indicators (KPIs) were developed by process along with the implementation of a process metric reporting system. However, linkage of compensation and incentives to process performance was not addressed as part of implementation, thus making it difficult for job performers to identify with process initiatives.

Conclusion – For process measures to be effective, individuals must be able to understand how their daily work contributes to the success of the process. They must be able to see a relationship between the results of the process and their compensation and incentives.

SCORING SUMMARY – PROCESS-BASED PERFORMANCE MEASURES

Figure 5.8 depicts that Process-based Performance Measures is the least mature of all the sections. Most of the organizations were in the beginning stage of understanding process-based measures and had limited success in their deployment. None of the organizations had any type of systematic approach for defining, communicating, or deploying process-based measures. The linkage of individual and process owner compensation to process performance was missing in all the case organizations.

Figure 5.8 Process-based Performance Measures

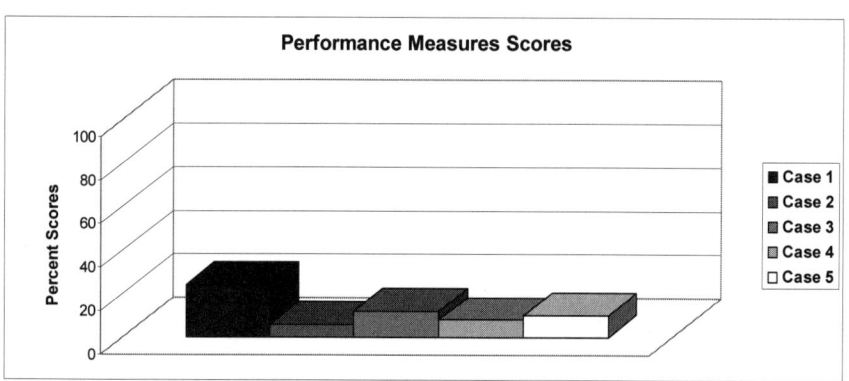

For Process Based Management to be sustained, process-based measures must be tied to compensation and other incentives. To achieve Process Based Management organization-wide, employees must understand and be rewarded based on their contribution to the successful execution of processes to meet customer expectations.

5.5.3 MIGRATION SECTION

The Migration category examines four characteristics to assess if an organization has a planned approach to migrate to Process Based Management.

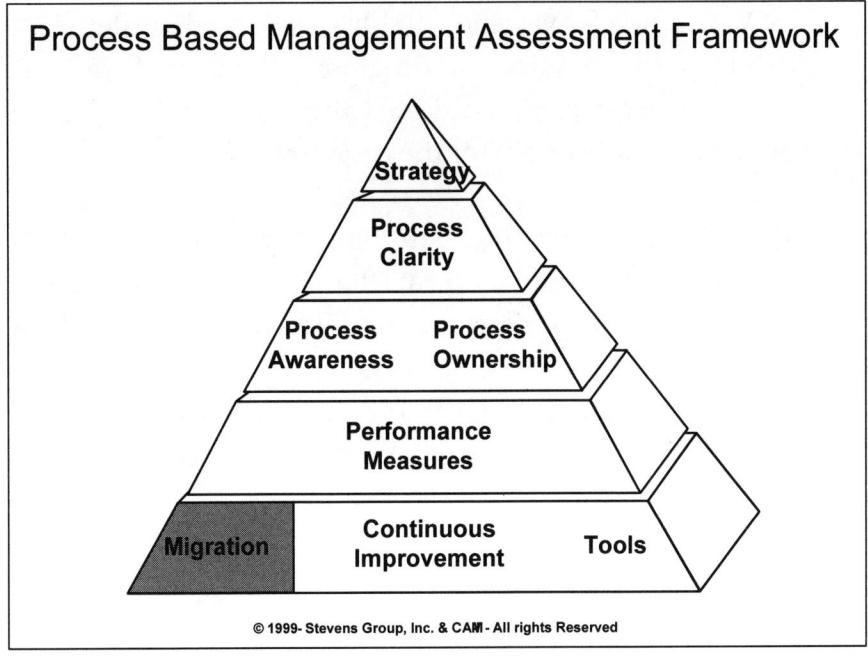

Process Based Management Assessment Framework

Strategy

Process Clarity

Process Awareness   Process Ownership

Performance Measures

Migration   Continuous Improvement   Tools

© 1999- Stevens Group, Inc. & CAM - All rights Reserved

MIGRATION KEY ITEMS

- *Transition Planning* - Examines if a transition plan has been built that defines the action plans required to move the organization from functional to Process Based Management. Also considered is whether the organization has defined a "process for process management" and, if so, how the process is kept current with changing environments.

- *Integration* - Determines if and how other types of initiatives have been integrated into the overall strategy for Process Based Management. Examines if the integration of methods and tools like ABC, Six Sigma,

ISO, Lean, TQM and Baldrige Award criteria to determine if these are stand-alone efforts or if they are part of a larger program that is aligned with the business model and philosophy of the organization.

- *Tools* - Evaluates the different types of tools, both technical and non-technical that are used to support Process Based Management. These tools could be software products for process analysis, improvement, and simulation, or they could be mechanisms for sharing best practices and communicating across different process teams or geographic locations.

- *Budget Linkage* - Identifies how process improvements are quantified and tied to budgets. Also included are how process improvements are evaluated and the method for funding the implementation of improvements (such as ad-hoc or self-funding versus a dedicated process improvement implementation budget). Finally, an assessment reviews how the process management program is linked to the budgeting and strategic planning processes.

MIGRATION CASE STUDY OBSERVATIONS

The key observation for Migration is that no case study organization had a "process for process management" or overall approach migrating current initiatives to Process Based Management. The case studies revealed the following key observations and associated conclusions:

- The integration of process initiatives was not coordinated and happened only through the efforts of internal facilitators. Also, there was no planned integration across processes. "We will be more successful if we can communicate the whole piece instead of the silo thinking operating with the different tool sets." The improvement process is people-dependent rather than process dependent; if the people leave, the effort would not survive.

  Conclusion – A well-defined and integrated "process for process management" is essential for migrating to Process Based Management.

- The migration to process management was led by Operations (vs. Finance) and was focused toward a balanced approach that includes quality, cost, and time performance improvements.   When the business transformation project was led by Finance it focused primarily on cost reduction.

  Conclusion – Migration should be cross-functional and strategic in nature, involving Operations, Finance, Strategic Planning, IT, and Human Resources, to name a few.

- A clear migration strategy and robust plan with detailed action plans had been developed but was not communicated beyond the small group that developed the plan. It had no top management ownership or buy-in.

Conclusion – The strategy to migrate to Process Based Management must be effectively communicated and have the appropriate buy-in and ownership to be successful. An aggressive, widespread communication and education program, beginning at the process owner level, must be implemented before any significant progress can be made

- Process owners were comfortable in their functional roles. The lack of a further mandate for process management and a process-based performance measurement system, make it difficult for any further progress to be made.

Conclusion – Process owners and teams must be in place and functioning as ongoing efforts (monitoring process performance and developing continuous improvements), with the authority and responsibility for leading change in the organization. Process owners have to be selected and have the authority and credibility to mobilize resources and commitment to change.

- Most of the organizations viewed their efforts as a one-time program or project with a defined start and end date. The priority was on programs and managing projects, not processes. The focus on projects limits the ability to keep the end-to-end process in the forefront of everyone's mind.

Conclusion –The focus must be on managing processes and the ongoing effort to migrate to Process Based Management.

SCORING SUMMARY – MIGRATION

The scores for the case study organizations indicated that Migration is being conducted on a limited basis. Only one organization demonstrated any type of a systematic approach toward Migration, the rest were all reactive or ad-hoc. Many of the organizations viewed their efforts as a one-time approach. Therefore, they did not address the key issues related to migrating to Process Based Management.

Figure 5.9 Migration

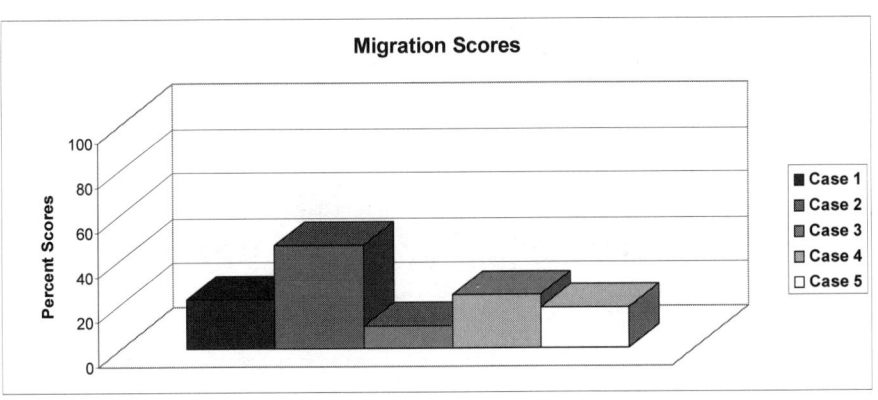

5.5.4 CONTINUOUS PROCESS MANAGEMENT SECTION

The Continuous Process Management category deals with the issues of continuous process improvement and how to embed Process Based Management into the organization so that it becomes the underlying philosophy.

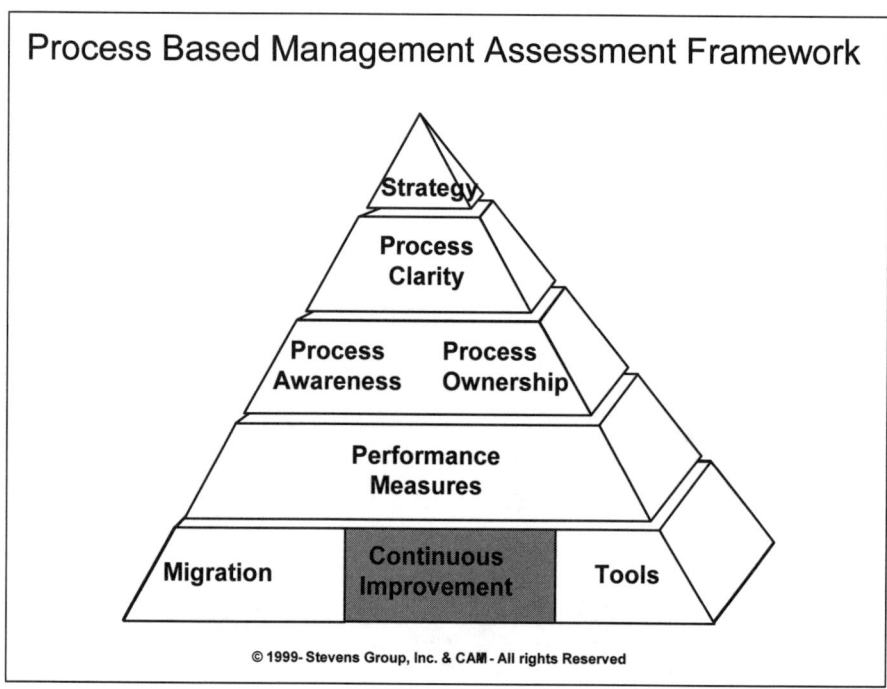

© 1999- Stevens Group, Inc. & CAM - All rights Reserved

CONTINUOUS PROCESS MANAGEMENT KEY ITEMS

- Continuous improvement efforts are reviewed to determine if they are part of the overall strategy, or initiated by specific events such as feedback from customers or employees.

- The extent that change management is incorporated and addressed as part of continuous improvement projects is reviewed.

- Cross-process integration and how it is achieved is addressed in this category. This includes how teams communicate changes across different processes and geographical locations so that they have consistent deployment plans.

- The methods and tools used by teams to identify improvement areas are identified and evaluated along with the approach for how process performance is monitored and communicated.

CONTINUOUS PROCESS MANAGEMENT CASE STUDY OBSERVATIONS

Many organizations had some type of continuous improvement program, but very few were linked to the strategy. None of the organizations had a formal change management program incorporated into their continuous improvement efforts, which resulted in limited success trying to embed Process Based Management. The case studies revealed the following key observations and associated conclusions:

- There is an imbalance of time spent gathering data rather than improving processes. The performance report card in one organization has 90 pages of data charts. The one-page Executive Summary has nine descriptive bullet points. None of the bullet points address process improvement. Metrics do not drive or prioritize Continuous Improvement efforts.

Conclusion – To embed Process Based Management into the organization, measures need to focus on the "health" of the process and use the results of process measures to drive continuous improvements.

- The overall strategy addressed continuous improvement by stating "Strive to develop a reputation for innovation and exemplary business practices…" and "To become institutionally agile and adaptable…" There was little detail in the operating plan or action plans on how to accomplish this.

Conclusion – For Process Based Management to be successful, a well-defined strategy and resulting operating plan that addresses continuous improvement needs to be in place and linked to employees' objectives.

- Many of the initial improvement opportunities were based strictly on their potential financial impact and were mostly functionally focused.

Conclusion- Improvement ideas need to be a result of the direction in the strategy and accomplish the key objectives of the strategy.

- No dedicated time to work "on" the process (improvement) versus "in" the process. Time was spent on fixing the process rather than improving the process.

  Conclusion – Management must allocate and support dedicated time for individuals to work on improving the process. Otherwise, organizations end up fixing the same problems over and over again.

- Areas of improvement were identified by using a suggestion system, sharing of best practices, and reviewing lessons learned. Each program used lessons learned from the knowledge management databases wherever possible.

  Conclusion – A mechanism needs to be in place for employees to provide feedback to process owners. Process teams need to share both lessons learned and best paratices, along with solutions that may affect other processes.

SCORING SUMMARY - CONTINUOUS PROCESS MANAGEMENT

The scores for this section are indicative of organizations just beginning their journey toward Process Based Management. Most of the organizations either had ad hoc improvement programs or were reactive at best. One organization did have the early beginnings of a systematic approach, with standards for communicating and driving improvements based on strategy.

Figure 5.10 Continuous Process Improvement

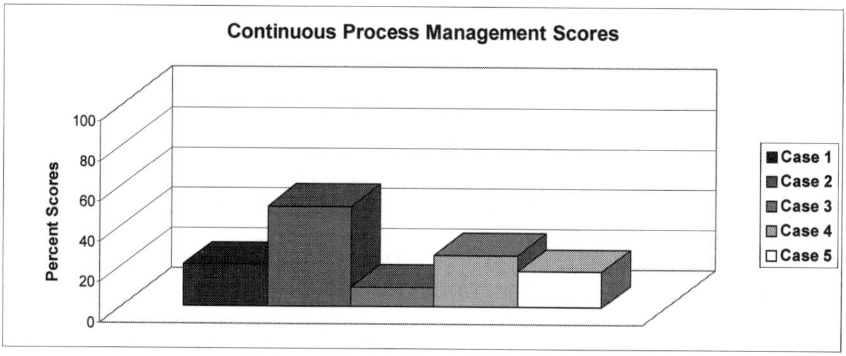

5.6 WHAT THE RESEARCH REVEALED

What did all the results from the case studies reveal in terms of Process Based Management?

- The framework established in The Road to Excellence is valid for all types of organizations

- For mindset change to occur, an organization must adopt a long-term perspective. Many of the case-study companies viewed their efforts as a one-time program or project with no integration into their long-term strategy. Without a linkage to strategy, an organization's process-based efforts will be short-lived, and subject to quick replacement by the next management fad that comes along.

- As Figure 5.11 indicates, Performance Measures is the most challenging aspect of Process Based Management to implement. It is also the area that takes the longest to see results. Even in those organizations that scored well in other sections, success was limited due to the lack of linkage of process performance to compensation and incentives. Employees were unable to see a link between the work they performed on a day-to-day basis and process performance.

- Successful integration of initiatives requires a "process" for implementing and sustaining process management. This should include linkage to the various initiatives underway. None of the case study organizations had an integrated, systematic approach that included cross-initiative representation.

- To embed Process Based Management into day-to-day operations requires a tie between strategy and the identification and prioritization of improvement programs and projects.

Figure 5.11 Overall Process Based Management Scores

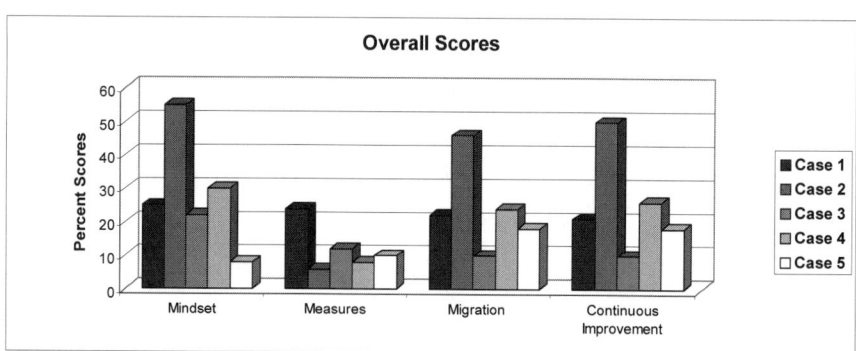

SUMMARY

It was also clear from the case studies, and our discussions with many other organizations that organizations need a mechanism to understand where they are on the journey to implement Process Based Management. They also wanted to understand what they should expect to see as they progress. This realization led to the development of the Process Continuum Model, which we cover in the next chapter.

CHAPTER 6:

THE JOURNEY: PROCESS CONTINUUM MODEL

OBJECTIVE:

Identify the attributes and characteristics an organization would expect to see as it moves along the journey to become process-based, presented in a framework called the Process Continuum Model.

An organization's transition from a functionally-oriented mindset to a Process Based Management mindset is difficult. The journey along the "Road to Excellence" is long and is not marked with clear milestones. The transition is more of a continuous period of development and change.

It became evident in conducting the case studies and from discussions with other executives and researchers that organizations evolve as they become process-based. As a result, there is a need to describe to organizations and managers what to expect as they move along the Process Based Management path.

The Process Continuum Model[38] was developed to capture organizational characteristics that should be evident during the transformation to Process Based Management. There are four levels of process development within the continuum:[39]

Figure 6.1 Process Continuum Model Levels

Process Continuum Model Levels

Level 4	Sustained
Level 3	Repeatable
Level 2	Defined
Level 1	Ad Hoc

---

[38] The Process Continuum Model is an adaptation of the Metric and Maturity model developed by Texas Instruments. *Metrics: A Management Guide for the Development and Deployment of Strategic Metrics*, Texas Instruments Incorporated, 1997.

The primary attributes of each level can be summarized as follows:

Figure 6.2 Summary of the Continuum model levels

Process Continuum Model		
Level 4	Sustained	Process Based management is firmly embedded in the organization. Employees are empowered to respond to customer needs. Position descriptions detail process roles, responsibilities and incentives. Processes are managed proactively in an atmosphere of continuous improvement.
Level 3	Repeatable	Integration is evident. The organization's identity, priority, mandated, and background processes are mapped at a detailed level. Process thinking has taken hold. Employees know their role in process and process teams are formed.
Level 2	Defined	High-level process maps exist within a classification framework. Measures are no longer only financially oriented. Recognition of the importance of process management is widespread. Process leaders are identified and roles defined. Employees are getting an understanding of end-to-end processes.
Level 1	Ad Hoc	The organization is functionally oriented with limited cross-functional understanding. A clear strategy may exist. However, there are no links between strategy, functions and metrics. There are pockets of process thinking.

The continuum model expresses the attributes an organization will demonstrate at each level based on the seven categories in the Process Based Management Assessment Framework presented in Chapter 5. Each level is made up of a series of characteristics reflecting the organization's process-oriented development. An organization is said to have reached a continuum level for a particular category after demonstrating a majority of the attributes at that category level - in addition to those of the preceding level.

The objective of the model is to help an organization understand what characteristics it can expect to see as it moves along the continuum. Characteristics are identified by levels, showing what should be in place to move to the next level. The continuum model is targeted at organizations and individuals who have experience with managing processes, and the Process Based Management concepts presented in *The Road to Excellence*.

This model works in conjunction with the other models in the Process Based Management Loop:

- Discipline model, which identifies the initiatives, methods, and tools in place in an organization and how they support and are aligned to the philosophy and business model of the organization
- Process Based Management Assessment Model, which provides a baseline of where the organization is today.

The Continuum Model identifies the characteristics needed to attain the next level. An organization would use the Discipline Model and the Assessment Model to gauge its situation. It would then develop action plans based on those insights, and the attributes in the Continuum model to get to the next level. An organizations philosophy and strategy will determine the level of the Continuum model that the organization should strive to attain.

Figure 6.3 Process Based Management Loop

Process Based Management Loop

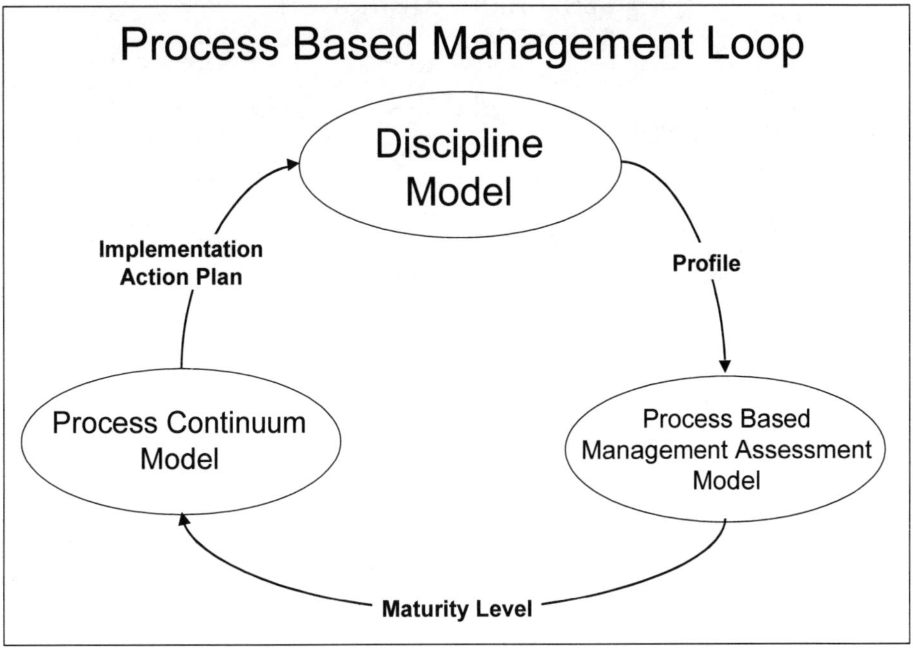

6.1 THE PROCESS CONTINUUM MODEL

The Process Continuum Model utilizes the seven categories shown in the Process Management Assessment Framework.

Figure 6.4 Process Based Management Assessment Framework

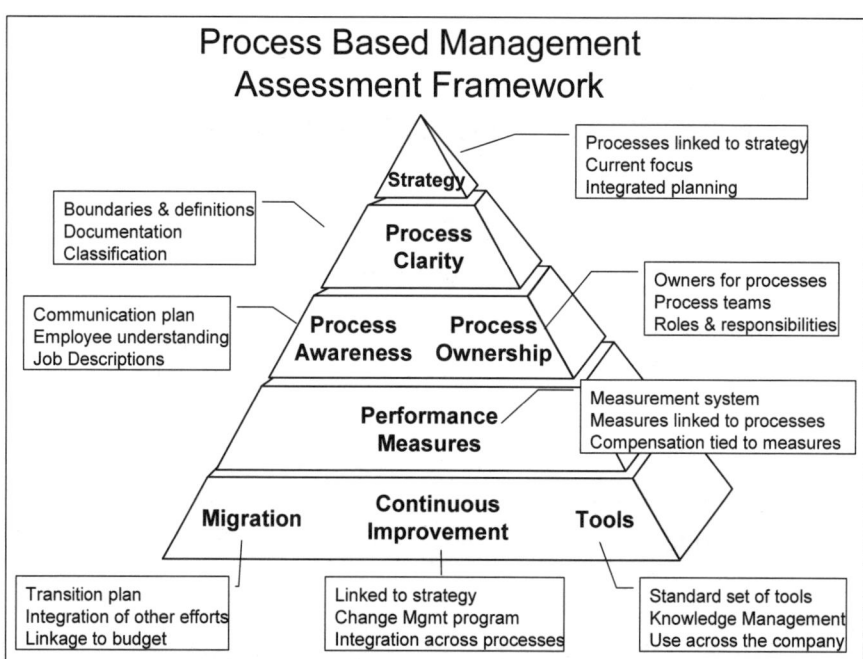

What you would expect to see in an organization at each of the four levels, by category, is presented in the next sections. The complete model for each of the levels is presented in a table in each section.

6.1.1 LEVEL 1: AD-HOC

At the ad-hoc level, the organization is functionally based with small pockets of process thinking.[40] The organization

---

[40] Relevant tools will be identified to support the process initiative at each level

has a strategic plan and has some understanding of its markets. There is no recognition of process as a strategic initiative. The organization may be using tools such as Economic Value Added (EVA) to measure its performance and Activity Based Costing (ABC) to identify and attribute costs. However, these are standalone initiatives not linked to strategy or any defined philosophy of how the organization will operate.

At this level, there is limited awareness, understanding, or clarity of processes. Even though the organization's focus is on functions (or departments), there is some understanding of activities within those functions. However, awareness of how work is performed continues to be functionally oriented. As a result, there is limited process training. Any process mapping is focused on the activities within functions, or at best, on independent processes. A function may have developed a relationship map that shows how an input comes into the organization and passes through the various functions to produce an output for a customer.

Process ownership is limited, if it exists at all. Any process teams are ad-hoc, with a functional team structure and functional roles and responsibilities. The lack of process structure limits the ability to change processes outside the control of a functional area. As a result, continuous improvement efforts are functionally oriented, focusing on the current pain.

Performance measures are primarily financial, with limited nonfinancial measures. These measures are functionally oriented, with little (if any) connection across functions, or processes. The measurement data is used only for control purposes, supporting the financial reporting efforts. Management reporting focuses on variances of actual results to a relatively static budget; this is also the basis for any incentive compensation.

An individual or group, however, has identified the benefit of a process-based focus. They see the negative effects of the disconnected initiatives, often driven by crisis. Even with limited process understanding, some processes are being managed, but with limited understanding of how to do it, or even awareness that they are the process champions. However, the seed has been planted, and those employees that understand the benefits of a process perspective are beginning to get together and discuss how to move this thinking forward. They may have formed an informal process group to periodically meet to discuss approaches and ideas. They have begun to plan how to link the various initiatives together, and they see Process Based Management as a way to accomplish that linkage.

6.1.2 LEVEL 2: DEFINED

At the defined level, the group of process believers has moved process thinking to a broader audience in the organization. There is now some discussion of processes in the strategy and operating plans. The processes that support

Level 1: Ad-hoc

Strategy	Clarity	Awareness	Ownership	Measures	Migration	Continuous Improvement
• Strategic plan is developed • Markets are understood • Functions are managed • Basic competencies are identified • Mission and vision are defined	• Functions are clearly understood • Relationship maps are in place • Functional activities are focused • Process documentation is limited • Processes are not classified	• Functions are understood by employees • Just-in-time and/or ad-hoc process team training is provided; focused on functions • Recognition is functional goal-based	• Ad-hoc process teams are used • Business practices are reviewed by functional owners (ad-hoc) • Functional team structure is used • Functional roles and responsibilities are defined	• Some non-financial measures are used • Measures, primarily gauging efficiency & output quantities, are internally focused • Primarily financial measures (cost, revenue, profit, ROI, etc.) are used • Measurement data are used for control, frequently for punitive purposes • Measurement efforts are functionally-oriented, disconnected among processes and across functions • Incentive compensation is tied to quotas & quarterly functional targets • Reporting is variance-based, focused particularly on actual versus an annual or relatively static budget, • Some non-financial measures are used	• Advantages of process management focus are identified • Initiatives are disconnected • Process focus is crisis driven • Improvements are crisis driven	• Improvement opportunities are reactively identified • Improvements are functionally-focused • Only functions and activities are costed • Improvement initiatives are disjointed • Improvements are narrowly- focused • Tools are randomly-used • A process improvement plan is not emphasized • Disconnects are not identified (causing frustration)

the vision and mission are defined. The Identity and Priority processes for the organization have been identified, with discussion of how these are supported by the organization's core competencies.

A scorecarding tool has been developed to communicate and implement strategy. A strategy map (developed as part of the Strategic Management process) makes it clear how the various initiatives support the growth and improvement aspects of the strategy. Customer and employee feedback, as well as benchmarking and possibly target costing, are used to develop the strategy and operating plans.

Processes have been defined at a high level, with a classification framework in place to provide a context showing how all the processes fit together. As a result of process thinking being included in the strategy and the development of a classification framework, there is an understanding and focus on processes across the organization. Clear process documentation is available to all employees, although it is not widely used.

To move from the emphasis on functions to an understanding of processes, a formal process training program is in place to increase employee understanding of processes. Management recognizes the importance of process thinking by explicitly recognizing process performance. Employees see that this new way of performing is what management will manage and recognize. But what holds it all together is the Process Owners, who are identified for each of the major processes. With the Process Owner's roles and responsibilities clearly identified, a process team structure evolved quickly. Teams are managing each process, and act based on balanced measurement information that is captured as part of the strategy process and the measurement systems in place.

At the defined level, the organization has moved from having some nonfinancial measures to a balanced set of measures that cascades from the strategy to what the process teams do and manage on an ongoing basis. These measures address the multiple dimensions included in a Balanced Scorecard[41] or similar measurement framework. This approach to measurement allows process teams to consider customer requirements and outputs, as well as the time, cost, flexibility and quality attributes of each process. The feedback received from ongoing customer and employee surveys is invaluable in allowing issues to be addressed before they become larger problems. Lagging indicators have been supplemented with leading indicators, which are much easier to identify now with the increased understanding of processes.

---

[41] Kaplan, Robert S. and Norton, David P., *The Balanced Scorecard ;* Boston, MA, Harvard Business School Press, 1996

Level 2: Defined

Strategy	Clarity	Awareness	Ownership	Measures	Migration	Continuous Improvement
• Strategy is clearly articulated • Identity and Priority processes are identified (Keen model) • Some cross-functional processes are managed • Core competencies are identified • Mission and vision are process supported	• Processes are understood • High level processes are defined and documented • Processes are the focus • Clear process documentation is available to all employees • Classification framework is established	• Processes are understood by the employees • Formal process training program is established • Some recognition is process goal-based?	• Identity and Priority process teams are chartered • Process Owners and champions are identified • Cross-functional process team structure is used • Process roles and responsibilities are defined	• Financial and non-financial measures are used • Measures are customer focused • Measurement among (1) Dimensions, such as, balanced scorecard perspectives, and/or (2) cost, quality & speed are somewhat balanced • Some process measures are used for planning • Measurement is directly aligned with individual & functional objectives, limited process and functional linkage • Compensation is associated with process measures • Some leading (predictive) & lagging measures are used. • No explicit cause and effect linkage.	• Process panels and process teams are formed • Process vision with links to strategy and detailed project plan developed • Current level of process performance is assessed • Cost vs., benefit analysis is conducted • Process management process is developed	• Process improvements are implemented • Improvement focus is process based • Process attributes are costed • Targeted projects are funded • Improvement plan is defined • Continuous Improvement (CI) tools are identified • CI plan is communicated • Disconnects are identified

Process measurement data is a routine agenda item at all management meetings. Managers are getting better at using the measures when considering changes in plans. With process measures directly aligned with the strategy, the linkage of process measures to functional and individual objectives is beginning to evolve. Incentive compensation plans are also beginning to incorporate process measures and to consider process team performance as a portion of compensation.

At the defined level, the organization is migrating from a functional focus at the ad-hoc level to a process focus. The process structure is rapidly evolving, with Process Owners and teams forming with identified roles and responsibilities. With the increased level of process understanding, and evolving process measures, the organization routinely evaluates the current level of process performance, and targets specific processes for improvement using the standard continuous improvement tools now in place. With the increased development and use of process documentation, they have clearly identified the" white space" between the functions of the organization. As the organization identifies performance deficiencies, they are improving processes and the linkages between functions and processes. Now that there is a "process management process" in place, the organization knows how to manage processes, and they are getting better at it.

6.1.3 LEVEL 3: REPEATABLE

At the repeatable level, processes are understood to be the key to providing service to customers and managing the business. Processes firmly support the organization's strategy. The focus is on the organization's Identity and Priority[42] processes – those that make the main difference regarding how well its customers are served. The organization clearly sees the benefits of integrated processes; they have moved from managing the white space between the functions to managing the white space between the processes.

The organization has detailed process maps for all Identity and Priority processes. High-level maps have been developed for Mandated and Background processes, most of which are performed by external firms whose core competence lies in the specific area. Where the organization still executes its own Mandated and Background processes, process capabilities have been carefully matched to the needs of the customer or the stakeholder for which the process is being performed.

Employees, who are all members of process teams, understand their role in end-to-end processes. These roles as process performers are well understood, as all job descriptions are rewritten to consider the process role. Formal training programs bring any new team members, or new Process Owners, up-to-speed quickly on the defined

---

[42] Keen, Peter G.W., *The Process Edge: Creating Value Where It Counts,* Boston, MA: Harvard Business School Press, 1997, p.26-27.

roles and responsibilities of each. Best practice process behavior is widely understood because the organization is constantly recognizing best process performers.

The measurement system links performance measures to processes. These measures are driven by customer requirements, and are well-balanced and explicitly linked to defined process metrics. The relationship between functions, processes and measures is well understood and documented. There is a broad understanding of leading and lagging measures; correlation patterns have also been established among process measures to monitor trends. Process performance standards are established and are the principal basis of measuring performance.

Targets for process measures are a key component of the planning and budgeting that takes place on an ongoing basis. The organization has had sufficient experience working with and understanding the measures that have become part of the reward system. Portions of both the base and incentive compensation system are tied to process performance.

Level 3: Repeatable

Strategy	Clarity	Awareness	Ownership	Measures	Migration	Continuous Improvement
• Strategy is supported by processes • Identity and Priority process are the focus • Integrated/inter-related processes are managed • Core competencies linked to processes	• Cross-processes understood • All Identity and Priority processes are mapped in detail • Mandated and Background processes are mapped at a high-level. • Process documentation managed and updated on a continuous basis	• Jobs are described in terms of process • Employee role in end-to-end processes is understood • Majority of recognition is process goal-based	• Permanent process teams are chartered • Process Owner: accountable established and managed • Process team formation, structure and procedures are standardized and documented • Process executives, process directors, process coordinators and process panels are experienced	• Measures and processes are linked • Measures are driven by customer requirements • Balanced measures and defined processes are explicitly linked • Process measures are routinely used in planning, budgeting, and simulation • Functional, process and corporate measurement efforts are integrated • Base compensation is associated with process measures • Leading & lagging measurement is widely understood	• Best practice & benchmarking are used • Process performance measures and process performer accountabilities are defined and managed • Process performance standards are established • Strategic business case is prepared • Process management process is implemented	• Improvement opportunities proactively identified • Processes are optimized • Improvements in business plan are supported by process cost • Improvements are prioritized • Projects are self-funded • Gap closure is based on process attributes • CI tools are implemented and used • CI plan is implemented • Disconnects are addressed

Process Based Management is how the organization operates. Everything the organization does consider processes. Processes are understood and measures are in place to monitor how the processes are performing on an ongoing basis.

The organization is continually improving processes. Process improvement efforts are tied to process performance and survey results, and are incorporated into the operating budget. Methods only thought about before, such as knowledge management and scenario planning, are now part of the management toolset.

6.1.4 LEVEL 4: SUSTAINED

Process Based Management has become the organization's mindset. The process focus is thoroughly ingrained in the strategy. Actions and decisions in the organization are from a process perspective. The organization actively manages it's identify and priority processes. The process infrastructure (process owners, process managers and process teams) is identified in the organizational structure and in job descriptions. Employees no longer have to think about a process focus, it is how the organization operates; it is how things are done. The Process Based Management approach is embedded in the philosophy of the organization. There is a detailed and ongoing communication plan around processes.

The business strategy drives process improvement efforts. Process teams are established based on business results and strategy, and aligned with the classification framework, which captures all the processes in the organization. These teams are the cornerstone of the continuous improvement efforts, driving process improvement in line with the strategy to meet customer expectations

Process performance measures are a key part of the reward system, with incentives linked to process performance, and the budget linked to processes. Individual performance is measured mainly from the perspective of the process teams, and how well the team has performed as a unit. All rewards are closely tied to measurement. Further, relatively few measures are required due to the extensive understanding and validation of key process measures and corporate performance drivers. The primary purpose of measures at this level is continual learning. Measurement results, both objective and subjective, are widely shared, discussed and analyzed. The relationship between corporate strategy, processes and measures is widely understood and continually updated. Causation patterns have been established between process, output and outcome measures.

Continuous process improvement is embedded in the organization, and process thinking is embedded in the culture. Process measurement and redesign occurs continually as customer requirements and process capabilities change. The process teams are responsible for

Level 4: Sustained

Strategy	Clarity	Awareness	Ownership	Measures	Migration	Continuous Improvement
• Strategy is process improvement driven • Management by processes • Core competencies managed by process • Relationship among corporate strategy, processes & measures is explicitly understood	• Identity and Priority processes are managed proactively	• Communication is process based • Continuous improvement efforts are employee driven	• Process teams are established/ unestablished (based on business results and strategy) • Teams are identified in organizational structure and employee position descriptions	• Incentives and processes are linked • Budget and processes are linked • Measures are driven by customer, process and strategy • Few measures are required • Continual learning is driven by process measures. • Measurement results are widely shared, discussed and analyzed • Total compensation is closely tied to process measures • Explicit cause and effect among process measures is identified	• Process Based Management mindset is embedded in the organization	• Process performance is systematically evaluated • Processes are certified • Continuous Improvement (CI) tools are embedded in culture • CI is embedded in culture • Disconnects are continuously managed

the monitoring of process performance and implementing changes as they need to be made. A program is in place to certify processes, process teams, and process performers. This is very effective in both prioritizing improvement efforts and identifying the training required for teams and team members.

The employees of the organization, from the CEO and senior management team through the Process Owners and process performers, cannot imagine what it would be like to work in any other type of organization. Everyone is challenged and empowered to provide the right level of service to their customers. When they need to adjust, all performers know what to do, and do it. New employees have the biggest adjustment, because it is so different from what they are accustomed to.

6.2 APPLYING THE PROCESS CONTINUUM MODEL-AN IMPLEMENTATION ACTION PLAN

The Continuum model is the third model in the Process Based Management Loop. As the organization uses the output and insights from the Discipline Model and Process Based Management Assessment Model, the Continuum Model supports the development of action plans to address gaps in the implementation. As the organization determines strategically what level it will target in the model, action plans can be developed based on the attributes in each category to reach that level.

As a stand-alone model, an organization can determine its place on the Process Based Management continuum by developing a situational profile. The profile is developed by performing an organizational self-assessment using the Process Continuum Model attributes. That understanding can then be used to develop action plans to achieve process management goals, and to move the organization along to the next level. Emphasis can be shifted from over-developed to under-developed categories. Achieving and sustaining a balance between the categories is vital to successfully progressing along the continuum.

Periodically an organization should conduct self-assessments to monitor its progress transitioning to Process Based Management. By repeating the evaluation steps, action plans can be altered and modified to ensure balanced growth. The interval between self-assessments will be determined by the organization's strategy. Issues to consider include the level of effort devoted to transitioning, competing business issues, and personnel turnover. The key idea is to use the model as a way to continually evaluate and monitor how the organization is progressing in becoming a process-based company.

The organization will decide what continuum level provides the most value, based on the strategy and philosophy in place. It makes sense for most organizations to be at least at the Defined level. The strategic decision to move to the Repeatable, and eventually the Sustained level will be made by those organizations where Process Based

Management is the consciously chosen management approach.

SECTION 3

KEY LEARNINGS AND FITTING IT ALL TOGETHER

This section starts with a summary of key learning's (Chapter 7) from the case studies and the ongoing work of the Research Group. These learning's, and the example of how to apply (Chapter 8) the Process Based Management Loop, can serve as an action plan to advance Process Based Management in your organization.

CHAPTER 7:

KEY LEARNING'S FROM THE CASE STUDIES

OBJECTIVE:

Present key learning's from the case studies

In Section 1 of this book, we defined the management model we call Process Based Management, as well as its benefits to an organization. In Section 2, The Process Based Management Loop was presented, which allows an organization to assess how it is doing implementing Process Based Management and what actions can be taken to move the organization forward. The Assessment Framework, presented as part of the Loop, was validated and tested during the case studies. This chapter summarizes key learning's from the case studies. The learning's will help any organization as they move along the journey to becoming process-based.

The case studies validated the Process Based Management Assessment Framework developed in the *Road to Excellence.* The framework proved to be a comprehensive tool to evaluate how an organization was progressing toward becoming a process-based company. The framework provided the structure to get to the right level of detail to understand what was working, and where changes needed to occur as the organization moved to becoming process-based. The model was also adaptable to varied industries, including a supply chain organization with its cross-organizational processes. What the model demonstrated was that the key steps required to implement Process Based Management are relatively consistent across industries.

7.1 BENEFITS TO THE CASE STUDY ORGANIZATIONS FROM THE ASSESSMENT

All of the organizations identified significant benefits from the assessment and case study process:

- It provided an independent assessment of the Process Based Management implementation progress. The identification of roadblocks and obstacles that the organization had not been able to address provided leverage for the process champion to move forward. All of the organizations indicated that an independent assessment was beneficial.
- The identification of each organization's strengths and gaps was specific and realistic, providing unbiased third-party feedback that

each organization could apply to move Process Based Management forward.

- The assessment provided a framework that identified what areas and actions were required and critical to continue moving the organization toward Process Based Management; many of these areas had not been previously considered. The assessment provided the organization with a process that put key areas into perspective.
- The assessment feedback provided the process advocate(s) in the organization with specific ammunition to address the obstacles and develop action plans.

The case-study companies were surprised at the level of understanding that the case study team was able to achieve. The structure and depth of the assessment framework model consistently applied allowed the case study teams to target the right areas at the right depth. Some of these insights were not always comfortable for the organization. The assessment revealed roadblocks and politics that the organization had been unable, or unwilling, to address thus far in its efforts. As a result of the case study team discovering the roadblock, the organization could now confront that situation.

Several of the case-study organizations used the results to develop an agenda to move process-based thinking forward. Clearly defined gaps were identified and a consensus developed on how to become a process-based company. As a result, Process Based Management became a key part of the management approach, including the management of processes as a strategic objective of the organization. The case study effort moved these organizations forward.

Because some of the case study organizations did not develop action plans to address the gaps, they remained stuck at the "ad hoc" level, despite significant process efforts. The case study sponsor had done all they could to remove obstacles, but there was a lack of strategic alignment and widespread support in the organization. There was no clearly identified objective in the strategy or support in the organization's philosophy for a process-based approach. Process thinking had come into the organization as a method or tool, and was struggling to be elevated to a strategic objective. Under the current circumstances, there was a strong possibility that the process initiative would go by the wayside to join the other failed initiatives, if the process mindset issues were not addressed. There was clearly a lack of alignment with the organization's philosophy and business model.

7.2 IDENTIFIED KEY LEARNINGS

The case studies led the Process Based Management research team to identify specific key learning's that organizations need to consider in pursuing a Process Based Management approach. The following list can serve as an action plan to advance Process Based Management in your organization:

- ✓ Executive engagement and commitment is critical.
- ✓ A mindset shift is required.
- ✓ Process owners are required at a high level.
- ✓ Process Based Management needs to be embedded in the strategy.
- ✓ There needs to be a "process" for Process Based Management.
- ✓ Integration of initiatives is critical.
- ✓ There are multiple entry points to Process Based Management.
- ✓ Size of the organization does not matter.
- ✓ Process management shift requires a long-term perspective.
- ✓ Process performance measures are critical.
- ✓ Process maturity and metric maturity need to be in sync.

7.2.1 EXECUTIVE ENGAGEMENT AND COMMITMENT IS CRITICAL.

There are many strategic initiatives, methods, and tools competing for resources in any organization. The Bain study (Chapter 4) indicates that on average, every organization has around ten initiatives underway at any one time. None of these initiatives will survive long without top management support, which is true of any major activity or initiative in any organization. Grassroots efforts can only survive for limited periods of time. Senior management support is always on the top of any list identifying what is required to implement changes in an organization. How can senior managers effectively support so many initiatives?

The Discipline Model (Chapter 4) provides a filter for senior management to identify what is important, and where effort should be expended. The premise is that initiatives will not survive in the long-term without a link to the business model and philosophy of the organization. The concepts described in the Discipline Model provide a framework for senior management to identify what key initiatives, methods and tools would provide value to the organization. The model provides a framework for an organization to identify how to support and coordinate all of the methods and tools that are in motion, by tying them to the business model and philosophy of the organization.

It is essential that a holistic management model like Process Based Management become part of the philosophy of an organization. Otherwise, processes are managed as short-term control projects seeking incremental improvements with little or no impact on the mindset of the organization. Managing the organization by the organization's priority and identity processes is dramatically different from the traditional process/function/project mindset. To be part of the organization's philosophy, Process Based Management must be clearly understood, strongly supported, and sponsored with active engagement by senior management, or it will not succeed. Processes must be how they manage and monitor performance. Processes must be an essential part of the management review process, and the basis of questions asked by senior management of process leaders and process performers on an ongoing basis. If senior management does not have this type of focus, no one else in the organization will have it either. They will continue to manage the way they always have, which is from a functional, not from a process, perspective.

7.2.2 A MINDSET SHIFT IS REQUIRED

Process Based Management requires a different way of looking at how:

- Work is performed in the organization
- Employees are managed
- Performance is measured.

For this approach to be successful, process thinking must be imbedded into the mindset of all employees so that it becomes the way they act and work in the organization. A manager's mindset must encompass the identification of stakeholder needs and the vision, goals, and strategy for meeting stakeholder needs.

This shift is required at all levels, and it begins with a customer focus. All effective business strategies flow from listening and responding to the voice of the customer. The development of products and services results from responding to the voice of the customer. Processes address "how" work gets done in the organization to increase customer value.[43]

Senior managers have to constantly promote, discuss, and monitor process performance. "If you don't measure it, you cannot manage it" and "tell me how you will measure my performance and I'll tell you how I will behave" are phrases that capture the importance of measurements. The mindset shift starts with the articulation of key processes in the organization's strategy and the prominence of process thinking in the business model. Within this model, process thinking heavily influences the operating plan, and is the focus of the ongoing initiatives that flow from the plan.

At the process performer level, the workers need to understand the impact of their actions on the processes that create customer value. The goal is for employees to understand how the process works (inputs, steps, outputs, and metrics), and to be held accountable as part of a process team to achieve the stated process objectives and metrics. As they manage and monitor these metrics, process performers will be motivated to continually improve the process to meet the stated targets for the metrics. Employees have a clear idea of how "what they do" affects the performance of a process. More significantly, they are empowered as part of a

---

[43] Daly, Dennis C. and Tom Freeman, *The Road to Excellence: Becoming a Process-Based Company*, Bedford, TX: Consortium for Advanced Manufacturing-International, 1997, p.4.

process team to fix the problems they see and experience on a day-to-day basis.

The true challenge exists for the manager. From their perspective, they are responsible for implementing all of the initiatives identified in the operating plan. From their experience, they have seen initiatives come and go. They have to decide which ones having staying power and which will pass quickly. They also have to continue to run their areas and departments to achieve the objectives of the organization.

So what is in it for managers? By focusing on the customer, Process Based Management reduces complexity and aligns the organization's focus to make clear what is important and what should be focused on. It reduces the ambiguity that managers typically experience. It does make their jobs less complex by reducing process variability, thereby reducing the frustration and providing a consistent framework and focus that drives what they do.

In the end, the mindset shift moves everyone in the organization to focus on not what I do, but what do we do to provide the level of service to meet our customer's expectations. An organization serves customers using business processes to focus its strategies. Business processes define the work to meet those expectations, and the expectations of all stakeholders.

Who are those stakeholders? Not all stakeholders are equal.

- ✓ The customer is the predominant stakeholder. The value proposition begins and ends with the *customer* who has a need for a product or service and an expectation of quality and cost.
- ✓ The *employees* have the skills and commitment to meet those needs. Their performance determines the level and quality of services delivered to customers.
- ✓ *Management* must provide the structure and resources that enable employees to be most effective and efficient to meet the customer needs, and achieve the long-term vision of the organization.
- ✓ The *organization* must provide to the community a safe and supportive environment for the employees and their families, so that employees can focus on fulfilling their responsibilities and achieving their goals.
- ✓ The company funds it efforts through sales of ownership stakes to *stockholders,* who desire an adequate return for their invested dollars, and through borrowings from entities that require repayment of principal and interest.

The philosophy and business model of each organization has the need to adequately address each of these stakeholders if the organization is to survive long term.

7.2.3 PROCESS OWNERS ARE REQUIRED AT A HIGH LEVEL

The role of the process owner, similar to the manager of a function, is to:

- Provide the vision and future direction for the process
- Provide the necessary resources required by the process team so that the process can perform
- Remove obstacles for the process team to execute the process
- Set process performance measures and targets
- Develop the measurement system
- Assess process performance and progress
- Manage the interaction and white space between processes

This person must be high enough in the organization to accomplish this role. The process owner must be able to navigate the infrastructure of the organization, or the process team will not be successful.

Even when process owners are at a high level of the organization, their roles and responsibilities must be clearly outlined and understood. We saw examples where the process owners were at a senior level, but as one said to us, "I don't know how to act when my process hat is on". In that instance, the structure was form over substance. The process owners understood the value of the process approach, and knew that these processes needed to be managed. However, the organization had not developed the process-owners roles and responsibilities to the level where the roles were actionable and understood in the company. They had not put the structure in place to monitor the processes and manage the process teams.

In other examples, we observed organizations that had process owners who were actively managing and monitoring their processes. They had made strides in implementing the infrastructure that is required to support Process Based Management. Process owner meetings were held on a regular basis. Owners managed cross-process metrics, provided the vision for the process, and linked processes to strategy. These organizations were seeing the impact of monitoring processes and managing process teams. This had a significant effect on the performance of the organization, and the quality of products and services provided to their customers.

7.2.4 EMBEDDED IN THE STRATEGY

Process Based Management needs to be embedded in the strategy of the organization. This is not an initiative that is part of the operating plan one year, and not repeated the next year. It affects the focus of the organization and the products and services that will be offered.

How does this happen? This is dependent on the maturity of the organization. A start up business (or division) can be structured from day one with Process Based

Management as the focus of their strategy, embedded in the philosophy. This eliminates significant challenges (such as changing mindset or culture) that established organizations need to address. Process Based Management is embedded in the strategy based on the identified direction and needs of the organization, which was developed as part of the launch of the business. The launch of Saturn by GM illustrates this approach.

For established businesses, the approach will be very different. Before Process Based Management can become part of the philosophy of the organization (Chapter 4 - Discipline Model), the process-based approach must become a strategic imperative of the organization. The strategy needs to emphasize that the organization will manage its processes, and its portfolio of processes, to realize the overall vision, mission and competitive advantage of the organization. The strategy identifies the specific processes that are critical to meeting the objectives of the organization, and providing value to customers. As process thinking becomes embedded in the strategy, it begins to become part of the culture, and eventually becomes part of the overriding philosophy of the organization. The key point is that the process journey starts with strategy and evolves to become part of the philosophy of the organization. Once part of the philosophy, it becomes embedded in the strategy. This is consistent with the structure of the Discipline Model: the Philosophy changes and evolves slowly; it is the foundation of the organization.

7.2.5   PROCESS FOR PROCESS BASED MANAGEMENT

There is a need for a "process" for Process Based Management. As an organization moves along the road to becoming process-based, a migration plan is required to guide the way. This plan is the process for Process Based Management. Without it, the organization will not know how to react in order to sustain the effort when problems are encountered. Many problems and challenges will be encountered.

So what is this process? It details how an organization will move along this road. At GTE Telephone Operations, they had a simple one-page process map, which is summarized in Figure 7.1.

Figure 7.1 GTE Migration Plan

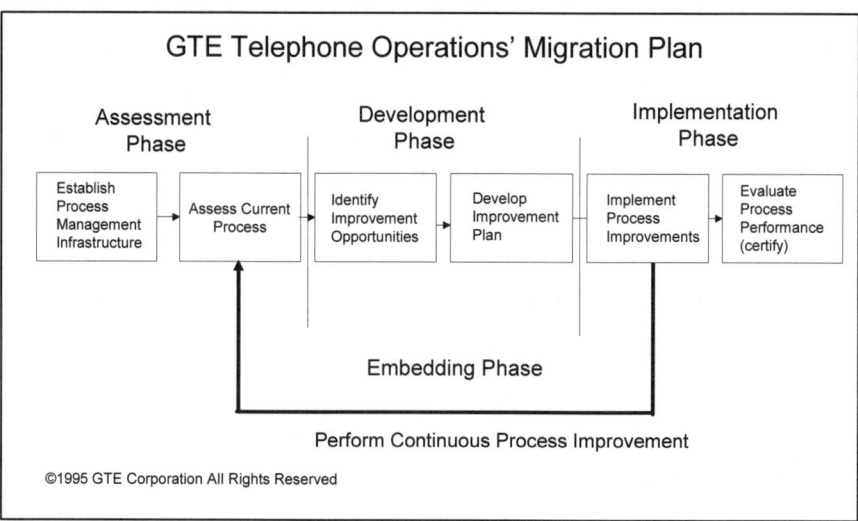

The implications of not having a clearly defined Process Based Management process became readily apparent in many of the case study companies. During the site visits, key players in the case companies saw that part of their challenge in moving forward (or not moving forward) was agreeing on, and implementing, this process. This process management process provides a migration path for an organization to follow.

7.2.6 INTEGRATION OF INITIATIVES IS CRITICAL.

The impact of having all employees and initiatives in an organization moving in the same direction is very powerful, and leads to superior performance. On the other hand, there is a significant negative impact of not having initiatives integrated and aligned to the philosophy and business model of the organization. Alignment is how organizations move in the same direction. A good example is how GE has focused on the "boundaryless" organization, Six Sigma, and digitization to align methodologies and tools. There are only a few critical areas that a company can focus on at any point in time (Refer to Chapter 4). If an organization tries to focus on too many areas and initiatives, the result is confusion, overlap, and eventually gridlock. The key is to align initiatives, methods and tools so they are clearly linked to strategy and are consistent with the management model contained in the philosophy.

For example, a strategy may be to continually improve a company's product and service offerings to its targeted customers; this is consistent with a management approach of Process Based Management. When we look at improvement initiatives that are used by organizations, we would link the improvement initiatives in use to Process Based Management, as shown in the following chart:

Figure 7.2 Integration of Improvement Initiatives

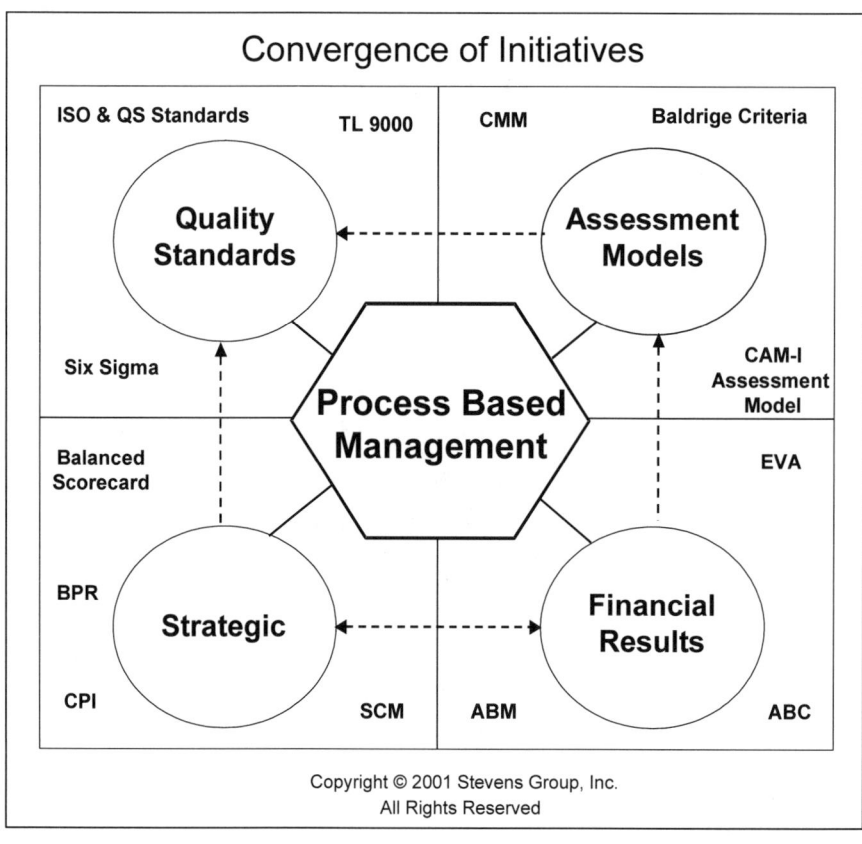

In this way, everyone in the organization can see how the methods and tools they are using support, and are aligned to, the management approach.

Process Based Management provides the framework to link these various initiatives, methods and tools together. Most of these have a process impact, or would greatly benefit from a process approach. Process Based Management as a management model is generic to industry; every industry would benefit to a certain degree from this approach.

7.2.7 THERE ARE MULTIPLE ENTRY POINTS TO PROCESS BASED MANAGEMENT.

All organizations start the Process Based Management journey at different points. It may have started with a reengineering initiative, Total Quality Management (TQM), or the many other methodologies and tools that organizations use. As organizations move forward, they realize what got them started needs to be part of a bigger picture, a philosophy supporting where the organization is headed.

The case study companies all started at different entry points:

- A reengineering initiative that reduced costs by over $1 billion but gutted customer service.

- The reality of decreasing budgets but continued demand for services, which required a better way to operate.
- A move to deregulation where customer service, reliable quality, and competitive costs would be the key to survival.
- The two ends of a supply chain that were trying to better manage and optimize that supply chain relationship.
- An impending privatization, which would require a renewed focus on the customer.

Each of these organizations was faced with a different situation. While each of these initiatives yielded results, the most effective results were attained when processes were affected. They all realized that a process-based approach would lead them in the direction they wanted to go. A process-based approach provided a clear path to a relentless focus on the customer. It was the best path for engaging the minds and dedication of their employees to the vision and mission of the organization.

7.2.8 SIZE OF THE ORGANIZATION DOES NOT MATTER.

The case studies observed organizations of significantly different sizes move toward Process Based Management. One case organization felt they were too large and another felt they were too small; they were both around the same size. Another case study involved entities which were a very small segment of their respective organizations. The assessment framework demonstrated that the same concepts and learning's apply to organizations of all sizes.

This is not to say that size is not an issue. Larger organizations are more complex and have more issues that need to be addressed. What we observed, however, is that the concepts and approach did not vary based on the size of the company. The difficulty and complexity of the implementation did.

The ideal size and situation for Process Based Management would be a startup organization. It has none of the mindset issues and could develop and implement an approach based on a clean slate, from a smaller base. Many of the issues and challenges faced by an organization that is trying to evolve to becoming process-based would not be present. An example here would be Southwest Airlines, which began operations in 1971 and developed a model from day one that we now recognize as being process-based.

Another example would be Saturn. It was developed as a new car company by GM, and was very successful for a short period of time. When GM brought Saturn back under its wings, problems mounted because of the different approaches of the two organizations. [44]

---

[44] Pfeffer, Jeffrey and Robert Sutton, *The Knowing-Doing Gap: How smart companies turn knowledge into action*; Boston: Harvard Business School Publishing; 2000 pages 81-93;

7.2.9 THE PROCESS BASED MANAGEMENT SHIFT REQUIRES A LONG-TERM PERSPECTIVE.

Process Based Management is a major change in how an organization will be managed and how work is performed. It is a change to the management approach in use at the company; this approach has evolved over time, and is not readily changed. It requires a change in the mindset of an organization, and that takes time. Texas Instrument's projected a ten-year implementation timetable to become a sustaining process-based organization. They never got there, due to divestitures and changes in management and direction.

This requires an organization to stay focused and to stay committed. An organization may not need to be at the sustained or perpetual levels of Process Based Management (based on the Process Continuum Model in Chapter 6). They may only need to achieve the defined or repeatable level. The point is that a mindset shift is essential to reach any level above ad hoc, and it will not occur over night. There are plenty of benefits that will be seen along the way to any level above ad hoc. The organization will see the benefits of getting better at managing individual processes rather quickly, usually within the first year.

As process measures are put in place and monitored over time, process performance will improve. As employees (process performers) understand their role in the processes, and execute their tasks in processes to achieve the stated process measures, they will be better aligned, and employee satisfaction and process performance will improve. The Process Continuum model depicts what an organization can expect to realize as they move along the path to becoming process based.

We cannot overstate the importance of a long-term perspective. It takes time and persistence to transform an organization, and to influence its philosophy. Management must be committed, and the message consistent, to earn the trust and commitment of the employees. They are watching to see if this is yet another initiative of the month. When they are asked to get involved and help improve their processes, they will watch to see how management reacts when they recommend process changes. When process owners are put in place, they will be watching if they really perform their role, or if this is another grab for turf and power in the organization.

When the employees see by management's actions that they are serious, the employees will stay on board, because it is a more challenging and empowering environment for an employee. They are now a performer on a process team, with clear expectations, and rewards tied to meeting measures that they were involved in setting. They have more control over providing the level and quality of service that will result in a satisfied customer. They have a more rewarding and challenging environment.

7.2.10 PROCESS PERFORMANCE MEASURES ARE CRITICAL

There are two sayings that we hear often. "If you don't measure it, you cannot manage it" and "tell me how you will measure my performance, and I'll tell you how I will behave". You get the performance that you measure. It should be understood that "You cannot measure what you do not define. And you cannot define what you do not understand."[45] To empower employees and teams to focus on performing and executing their process responsibilities, process measures need to be developed, implemented, and managed. But most importantly, the process performers and managers need to be accountable and rewarded based on process performance.

It is one thing to develop the measures. It is another to use them. We saw instances where one group had done a good job of developing process measures. They were detailed, specific, and all encompassing. The problem was they were developed in a vacuum, and not shared with the process owners, managers, and only in a few instances, the process performers.

It is critical that the process teams are involved in developing the process measures for their process. They need to consider the strategy of the organization, as well as

---

[45] CAM-I Capacity Interest Group, *Capacity Measurement & Improvement*, Chicago, IL: Richard D. Irwin, 1996, p.xiv.

the measures in place for other processes. If they develop the measures, and understand how the measure and the target are calculated, they will be well positioned to meet the measure. They understand how to improve the process to achieve the target measure that was established (and updated on a periodic basis). If they develop the measure, it is their measure to meet, not a measure that was dictated from on high. There is buy-in, and a win-win for the organization. If the process team meets the measure, which they were involved in developing, the organization performs well (the process is performing based on expectations) and the process team members are compensated accordingly (they met the performance measure which is tied to their compensation).

7.2.11 PROCESS MATURITY AND METRIC MATURITY NEED TO BE IN SYNC.

As process maturity in an organization increases, the metrics that measure those processes must continue to evolve in sync with the related process; and vice versa. The "TI (Texas Instruments) Metric & Maturity" model illustrates this:

Figure 7.3 TI Metric Maturity Model [46]

Metric & Maturity model				©Copyright 1996 Texas Instruments
Process Description	**Summary**	**Level**	**Summary**	**Metric Description**
Process management provides world class competitive advantage. (nodal influence – agility – forward looking)	Optimizing	**5**	Optimizing	Metric-driven actions are simulated during the strategy-setting process to ensure organizational alignment before metrics are implemented.
Supporting processes are integrated with and enable the core business processes to provide competitive advantage. Customer-focused process management is applied unconsciously.	Supporting Processes Integrated	**4**	Total Alignment	All metrics (process, results, organizational, geographic) are aligned with strategic objectives, provide competitive advantage, and optimize the whole.
Common process language and standards exist. Core processes are integrated to allow the seamless flow of work across process boundaries.	Core Processes Integrated	**3**	Horizontal Alignment	Metrics reinforce and leverage activities across all core business processes. Local interests are subordinated to the good of the whole.
Business process management, which begins and ends with the customer, is established, in control, and in management's conscious thinking.	Core Processes Managed	**2**	Vertical Alignment	Process metrics have been added and integrated with result metrics. Metric alignment between the strategy and daily activities in the core processes is established.
Little or no process focus. That which exists is primarily directed internally toward local operations.	Initial	**1**	Initial	Metrics are ad hoc and primarily results oriented.

This model was developed as an enterprise-level guide for assessing the maturity of an organization in process and metric management.

Here is an example form the TI guide. A core process related to product development activities is documented, in control (repeatable), consistently deployed across the enterprise, and has measurable improvement gains. This process is probably at or near level 2 maturity. If the metrics indicate variations in the process results, then they are still as level 1, because the process is not in control.

---

[46] Texas Instruments, *Metrics: A Management Guide for the Development and Deployment of Strategic Metrics,* Texas Instruments Incorporated, 1997.

If leading metric indicators predict results and influence activity, the process exhibits level 2 characteristics. When metrics also align with enterprise level strategic objectives (i.e., process users understand cause and effect relationships between what they do and enterprise success), then the process may be operating at level 2 maturity.

Developing, managing, and maintaining meaningful and actionable process metrics is not easy. As you understand and define the process, metrics are developed to monitor and manage the health of the process. This metrics are updated based on increasing levels of understanding and analysis of the cause and effect relationships that impact process performance.   As the process is improved, the metrics need to be updated to continue to provide the information needed to monitor and manage the process. It is ongoing effort to keep process metrics and process maturity in sync. Models such as the TI Metric Maturity Model provide frameworks for organizations to follow.

CHAPTER 8:

FITTING IT ALL TOGETHER

OBJECTIVE:

To provide an example of how the different Process Based Management models work

FITTING IT ALL TOGETHER

Now that you are familiar with the Process Based Management Loop (composed of the Discipline Model, Process Based Management Assessment Model and Process Continuum Model), let's review how an organization can use this loop to aid in the implementation of Process Based Management.

These management models closely interact with each other and should be used together. The **Discipline Model** provides a diagnostic profile that is used to represent the philosophy, business model, methods and tools an organization has deployed, and how these are linked.

The profile supplies critical information to the **Process Based Management Assessment Model**, which is used as a context to evaluate strengths and gaps in implementing Process Based Management. The results from the assessment are evaluated to determine the process maturity level of the organization, which is used as input into the Process Continuum Model.

Using the maturity levels for each category, the **Process Continuum Model** identifies the attributes an organization should have, or needs to obtain, to reach its targeted maturity level determined by senior executives. The organization then develops action plans to close the gaps. After implementing changes, the company assesses its progress towards Process Based Management by once again applying the Discipline Model. This iterative process is depicted in Figure 8.1 as the Process Based Management Loop.

8.1 EXAMPLE

We will use a fictitious company called CSO, Inc. to illustrate how the different models interact with one another. CSO designs, manufactures and sells outdoor furniture through catalog and retail centers across the United States. Their annual sales are approximately $400M and are growing at a 10% annual rate. They sell several different styles of outdoor chairs and tables, which customers order from account representatives. During the 25 years CSO has been in business, it has enjoyed strong customer loyalty, continued growth, and expansion.

Figure 8.1 Process Based Management Loop

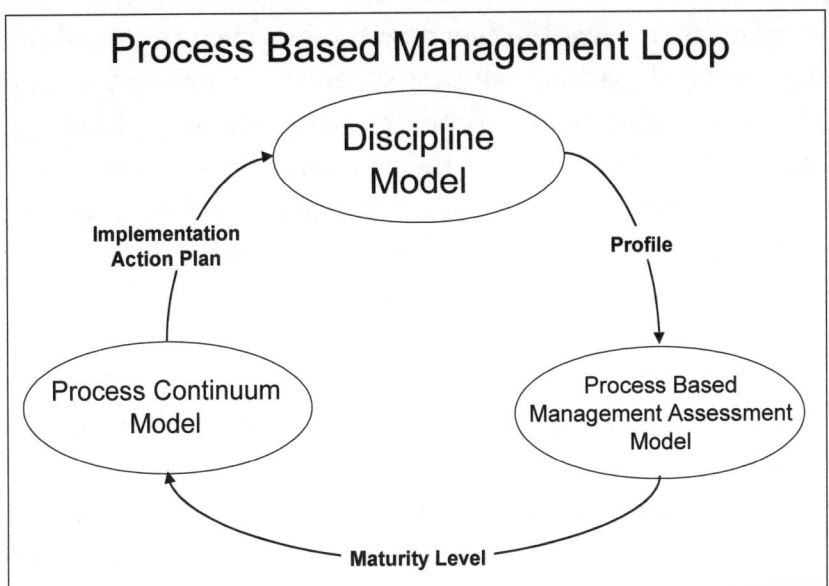

CSO is organized in a traditional function-based management structure with vice-presidents of Marketing, Product Development, Finance, Operations, and Manufacturing, all reporting to the CEO.

The past few years have seen the entry of new competitors in the outdoor furniture market with lower prices for comparable products of similar quality. CSO has also noticed a marked decline in customer satisfaction, but has not yet determined its primary causes.

The Company has a vision of providing the best overall value to its targeted customers. Its mission and values are consistent with that vision. Several departments at CSO have attempted to improve their performance using a variety of programs such as TQM, ISO, CPI and ABC. When each program is reviewed independently, it appears successful at improving departmental performance. However, overall customer satisfaction continues to decline. From an organizational perspective, the programs are not working. In addition CSO is planning to introduce a new line of custom made ergonomic outdoor furniture that would be available only through a new internet portal.

The newly appointed Director of Corporate Strategy realized that CSO needed an integrated approach to address customer satisfaction and service delivery issues. She realized that it would be critical to maximize the efficiency of CSO's processes rather than its departments for this new product line and internet process to be successful. The organization had been slowly transitioning from their department-based approach to a process-oriented approach. This transition was motivated by numerous management initiatives that had limited short-term success except when they affected processes. Many managers were having difficulty understanding their roles in terms of the processes in which they participate - rather than in terms of the functional groups to which they belong. This realization led the Director of Corporate Strategy to seriously consider the adoption and implementation of the Process Based Management Loop. She had been exposed to this topic after reading "The Road to Excellence - Becoming a Process-based Company" and attending several CAM-I CMS quarterly meetings devoted to process management research issues. CSO's adoption of the balanced scorecard was also a contributing influence. To support the effort, the Director created a pilot project to explore the Process Based Management Loop. This pilot team, which consisted of managers with process management experience from marketing, manufacturing operations, product development, information technology, finance and human resources, was responsible for developing an in-depth knowledge of the Process Based Management Loop by trying to apply the model to CSO. If they concluded that it was useful, they would determine what was necessary to implement Process Based Management, and to assist the organization to reach that objective.

8.2 GETTING STARTED – THE DISCIPLINE MODEL

The first thing the Process Based Management (PBM) Team did was to create a list of CSO initiatives, documenting:

(1) The year implemented
(2) The status of the initiative (whether it was still in place or was no longer being used); and
(3) Perceived employee reaction.

Figure 8.2 is an excerpt from the first matrix CSO built to capture all initiatives in place.

Figure 8.2 List of Initiatives

Initiative	Year Implemented	Status	Employee Reaction
TQM	1994	No longer used	A "Quality" Fad
Re-engineering	1995	No longer used	Job elimination, RIF
ISO 9000	1992	Still used for certification	Requirement for doing business
Cost reduction	1998	Used on an ad-hoc basis	More work, less people
Balanced Scorecard	1999	Still used	No understanding of how it affects my job

After analyzing the information from past initiatives, the PBM team developed the following timeline (Figure 8.3). It was used to facilitate discussions around the various programs' linkage to the corporate strategy included in CSO's business model.

Figure 8.3 Timeline for Initiatives

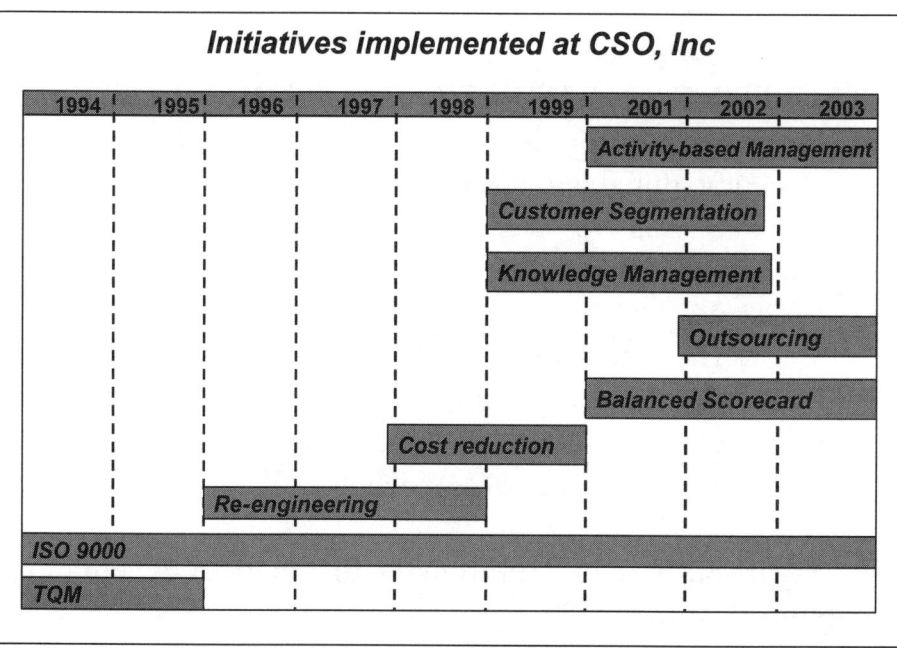

The PBM team then evaluated if its differentiation strategy was supported by the initiatives still being used, and if not, what "methods" would be best for implementing that strategy. Using the table in Figure 8.4, the team realized some parts of their strategy had limited initiative support, and some actually conflicted with their overall strategy.

Figure 8.4 Initiative support of strategy

Initiative	Strategy	
	Customer Focus	Low Cost
Balanced Scorecard	x	x
Knowledge Mgmt		
Customer Segmentation	x	
ISO 9000		
ABM		x

For example, initiatives underway in Knowledge Management and ISO 9000 did not directly support the current strategy.

From this information, the team built a detailed profile that included the following:

- Key products and services.
- Strategic challenges.
- Current and past initiatives.
- Key processes.
- Supporting methods and tools.

Analysis of the profile information indicated that CSO had an overriding management philosophy focused on customer service management, with some pockets of process-based thinking. Based on this, management determined that an assessment of their process-based efforts would be beneficial in terms of giving them direction on where to focus their action plans.

8.3 PROCESS BASED MANAGEMENT ASSESSMENT FRAMEWORK

To begin the assessment process, The PBM team designated a team of four individuals, in addition to their members, who were familiar with the key components of Process Based Management Assessment Framework defined in Figure 8.5. The team gathered data from all parts of the organization, and provided responses to each of the criteria items identified.

The PBM team reviewed all the completed responses with the team of assessors and determined that an external review would be beneficial. A third-party organization experienced in process-based assessments was engaged to evaluate the responses, identify existing strengths and gaps (Figure 8.6 is an example for Process Clarity), and recommend prioritized improvement areas for CSO.

Figure 8.5 Process Based Management Assessment Framework

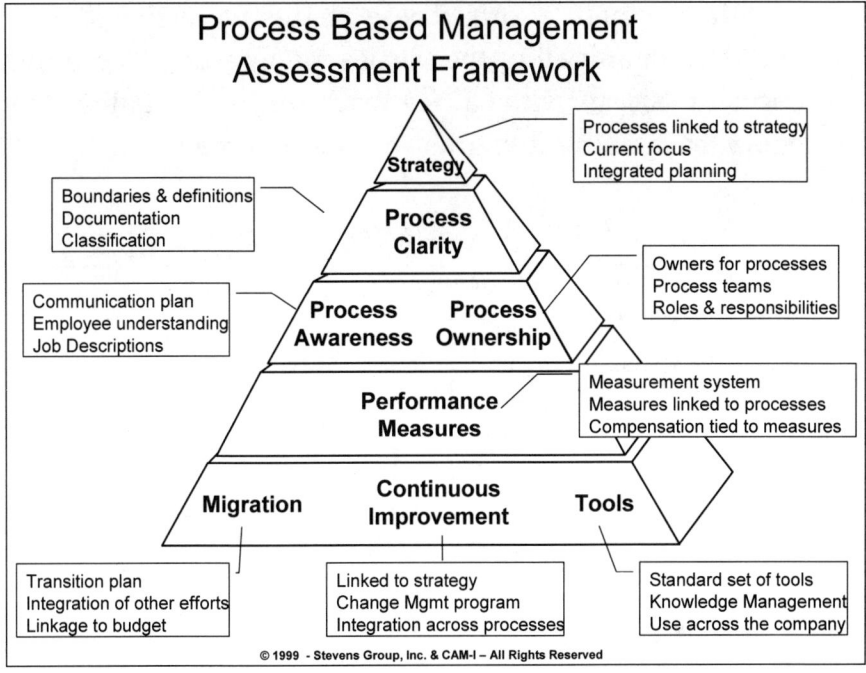

© 1999 - Stevens Group, Inc. & CAM-I – All Rights Reserved

Figure 8.6: Strengths and Gaps for Process Clarity at CSO

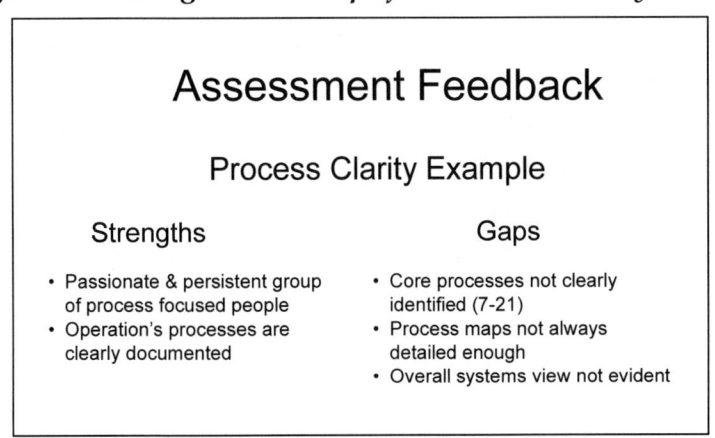

The third-party review produced the radar chart in Figure 8.7, which depicts the assessment of CSO's Process Based Management efforts. These results were shared with the PBM team and all of the parties who participated in the assessment along with a feedback report detailing, by category, each of the strengths and improvement areas.

Figure 8.7 Assessment Score

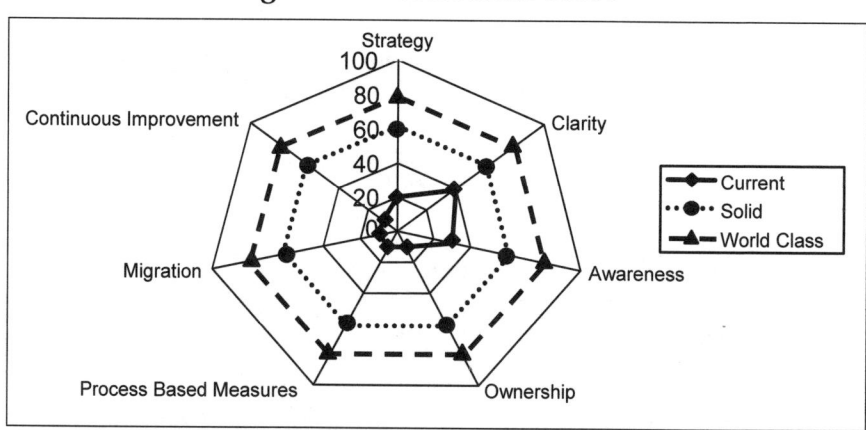

As part of the review, the scores in Figure 8.7 were converted into the maturity levels depicted in Figure 8.8. The maturity levels are based on the Process Continuum Model's four levels; Ad-hoc, Defined, Repeatable and Sustained. From the maturity levels, the PBM team determined they would need to focus short-term action plans on enhancing the process orientation of the Strategy, Awareness and Ownership areas as a starting point.

Figure 8.8 Maturity Levels

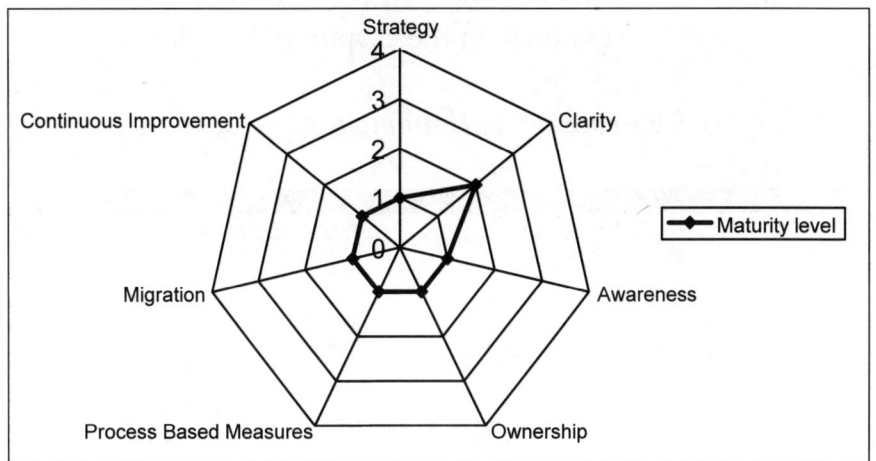

8.4 PROCESS CONTINUUM MODEL

Using the Process Continuum Model (an excerpt is provided in Figure 8.9), the PBM team built short-term action plans that would enable CSO to move from Maturity Level 1 to Level 2 for Strategy, Awareness and Ownership. As an example, an action plan was created to develop an overall communication plan that addressed the following key items:

- Develop a standard Process Based Management PowerPoint presentation to be used by all executives
- Assign each executive a division in which they will give the standard presentation and answer any questions
- Develop a monthly newsletter to communicate the efforts of process teams

- Give all employees easy access to process-based training materials (such as the output from all executive presentation sessions) on the corporate intranet

Figure 8.9 Process Continuum model – Levels 1 & 2

Category	Level 1 Ad hoc	Level 2 Defined
Strategy	Strategic plan developed	Strategy is clearly articulated
	Markets understood	Identity and priority processes are identified (Keen model)
	Functions managed	Some cross-functional processes managed
	Basis competencies are identified	Core competencies are identified
	Mission and vision are defined	Mission and vision are process supported
Process Awareness	Functions are understood by employees	Processes are understood by employees
	Just in time and/or ad-hoc process team training is provided; focused on functions	Formal process training program is established
	Recognition is functional goal based	Some recognition is process goal based
Process Ownership	Ad Hoc process teams are used	Identity and priority process teams are chartered
	Business practices are reviewed by functional owners (ad-hoc)	Process owners and champions are identified
	Functional team structure is used	Cross-functional process team structure is used
	Functional roles and responsibilities defined	Process roles and responsibilities defined

Each of the action plans developed would be assigned to an owner, and progress would be tracked on a monthly basis. Action plans would be completed, and new ones developed, on an ongoing basis. During ongoing strategy and operations reviews, the PBM team would reevaluate their progress moving to level 2 in the Strategy, Awareness and Ownership categories. The long-term objective of implementing Process Based Management as a management philosophy in the organization would be reviewed through a periodic self-assessment, thus starting the review cycle over again.

The PBM team concludes that the Process Based Management model was feasible to implement in CSO. The challenge now was how to gain organizational buy-in to implement PBM organization wide.

Throughout this book we have emphasized that taking a process based management approach is the key to competitive advantage. Process Based Management is a journey, not a destination, and the organization that continues to develop and understand its processes is best able to learn and improve customer value.

This research leading to this book is an attempt to develop a set of prescriptive models that will lead your organization to attain competitive advantage. Apply the Process Based Management Loop to your organization. Let us know what you find, and where you think these models can be improved. The goal is to provide approaches and models that process-based organizations will find helpful in moving toward Process Based Management. Continuous improvement of these models will help us reach that goal. We look forward to your insights and feedback.

Pat Dowdle	Jerry Stevens
pat@processadvantage.com	jerry@stevensgrpinc.com
847-501-4319	919-471-9029
Bob McCarty	Dennis Daly
mccarty@fincen.uscg.mil	dennis.daly@metrostate.edu
757-523-6705	612- 659-7295

Appendix A:

GLOSSARY

ABC - Activity-based costing - A methodology that measures the cost and performance of cost objects, activities and resources. (Source: CAM-I Glossary)

ABM - Activity-based management - A discipline focusing on the management of activities within business processes as the route to continuously improve both the value received by customers and the profit earned in providing that value. ABM uses activity-based cost information and performance measurements to influence management action. (Source: CAM-I Glossary)

Activities - Work performed by people, equipment, technologies or facilities. Activities are usually described by the "action-verb-adjective-noun" grammar convention. (Source: CAM-I Glossary)

Attributes - A label used to provide additional classification or information about a resource, activity, or cost object. Used for focusing attention and may be subjective. (Source: CAM-I Glossary)

Balanced scorecard - Translates an organization's mission and strategy into a comprehensive set of performance measures that provides a framework for a strategic measurement and management. (Source: Kaplan and Norton, *Balanced Scorecard*)

Baldrige criteria - Seven areas: Leadership, Information Analysis, Strategic Planning, Human Resource Development & Management, Process Management, Business Results, Customer Focus & Attention. (Source: Baldrige National Quality Award – NIST)

Benchmarking - A systematic and continuous measurement process; a process of continuously measuring and comparing an organization's business processes against business process leaders anywhere in the world to gain information which will help the organization take action to improve its performance. (Source: APQC)

BPR - Business Process Reengineering. Also refer to **reengineering** - The radical redesign of a process, product or service (as opposed to the incremental improvement associated with continuous improvement efforts). The objective of a re-engineering strategy is to simplify processes, products or services in order to become more responsive to the customer. (Source: Daly and Freeman, *Road to Excellence*)

Business model - A simplified representation of a business, with any hypotheses required to describe or explain the business, often expressed mathematically.

CAM-I Assessment Framework Model Also refer to **Process Based Management Assessment Framework -** A set of criteria used to evaluate an organization's maturity implementing process based management.

CMM - Capability Maturity Model - (1) A structured, conceptual framework that defines the management of software development and maintenance processes; (2) a management tool for software and IT organizations to systematically improve their development and maintenance processes. (Source: Gabriel Pall, *Process Centered Enterprise*)

Characteristics - Distinguishing features or qualities of a process or its output on which variables or attributes can be collected.

CMS – Cost Management Systems - A system of tools, methods and techniques for the management and control of cost and resources. The resulting information will have utility in setting and evaluating the organization's strategies.

Continuous process management - A program to manage business processes to achieve or improve a desired result (reduce waste, reduce response time, simplify the design of processes, and improve quality. (Source: Daly and Freeman, *Road to Excellence*)

CPI – Continuous process improvement - A program to eliminate waste, reduce response time, simplifies the design of both products and processes, and improve quality. (Source: CAM-I Glossary)

Cross-functional - The interdepartmental coordination that crosses levels of hierarchy and formal boundaries committed to a common purpose to realize the goals of an organization. (Source: Daly and Freeman, *Road to Excellence*)

Customer value - The difference between customer realization and sacrifice. Realization is what a customer receives. It includes product features, quality, service and cost to use, maintain, and dispose of the product or service. Sacrifice is what the customer gives up, which includes the amount the customer, pays for the product/service plus the time and effort spent acquiring and learning how to use the product/service. Maximizing customer value means maximizing the difference between realization and sacrifice. (Source: Daly and Freeman, *Road to Excellence*)

Department - A division of a business enterprise dealing with a particular area of activity: *the human resources department.*

Discipline model - An approach to identify how initiatives, methods and tools are aligned with the strategy and the philosophy of the organization.

End-to-end process - An organized set of activities that interrelate with each other and defined as a whole with defined inputs and outputs that cannot be divided into independent parts to accomplish a specified objective.

EVA (Economic Value Added) - After-tax return on invested capital, less the cost of that capital.

Function - A division of an organization organized to perform a specified action or activity.

Functionally-focused organizations - An organization that is organized by specific functions such as accounting, production, and sales. (Source: Daly and Freeman, *Road to Excellence*)

Governance - A system of management and controls exercised in the stewardship of an organization. It includes responsibilities of the owners/shareholders, board of directors, and CEO. (Source: NIST Baldrige Award Criteria)

Holistic - The view that fundamental components of reality, have an existence independent or greater than the mere sum of their parts.

ISO standards - A series of standards relating to quality assurance and quality management that companies must meet in order to be certified by the International Organization for Standardization. (Source: Society of

Management Accountants of Canada, *Becoming ISO 9000 Registered)*

Knowledge management - Techniques and practices for enhancing an organization's ability to capture, utilize, codify and develop knowledge consistent with the organization's mission and strategy. (Source: Society of Management Accountants of Canada)

Lagging indicators - Measures that report the outcomes or consequences of past actions. Frequently financial measures.

Leading indicators - Measures that report on the drivers of future performance.

Model - A simplified representation of some real world phenomena.
Quantitative model is a set of mathematical relationships. A descriptive model specifies the relationship between a series of independent and dependent variables. Optimizing models suggests a specific choice between decision alternatives.

Nonvalue-added activity - An activity that does not contribute to customer value or to meeting an organization's needs. The designation non-value-added reflects a belief that the activity (or process) can be redesigned, reduced or eliminated without reducing the quantity, responsiveness, or quality of the output required by the customer or the organization. (Source: CAM-I Glossary)

Philosophy - A system of principles for guidance in practical affairs. The vision, mission values, and management approach which is the foundation for providing value to the stakeholders of an organization.

Process - A series of activities that are linked to perform a specific objective. (Source: CAM-I Glossary)

Process Based Management - A management approach that focuses on:
- Promoting a process based culture
- Managing end-to-end business processes to continuous improve cost, time, quality and flexibility of products and services to customers
- Understanding and meeting customer expectations
- Integrating diverse initiatives into a process-oriented approach
- Linking incentives and compensation to process performance.

Process Based Management Assessment Framework - A set of criteria used to evaluate an organization's maturity implementing process based management.

Process-based organization - An organization that manages the enterprise with the explicit recognition and management of business processes undertaken to meet, or exceed the organization's stakeholders' needs with the customer being the predominant stakeholder. (Source: Daly and Freeman, *Road to Excellence*)

Process-based performance measures - Indicators of the work performed and the results achieved in an activity, process, or organizational unit. Performance measures may be financial or non-financial. (Source: Daly and Freeman, *Road to Excellence*)

Process centered organization - An organization, at any level, in which the business process is the defining organizing concept for structure, resource deployment, and management. (Source: Gabriel Pall, *Process Centered Enterprise*)

Process classification - A basic analytical tool for determining which processes deserve attention and investment. (Source: Peter Keen, *Process Edge*)

Process champion - The individual responsible for defining the scope of the project and identifying critical sub-process business issues. The process champion should also create the permanent process team, serve on the process panel, champion the sub-process team, and provide team rewards and recognition. (Source: Daly and Freeman, *Road to Excellence*)

Process Continuum Model - The attributes and characteristics an organization would expect to see during its migration to Process Based Management are captured at the four levels (ad hoc, defined, repeatable, and sustained) of the model.

Process council - A cross-functional executive team responsible for providing alignment across processes, integrating process improvements across functions, reallocating resources to fund action plans, and providing clear line of sight to customer needs.

Process hierarchy - A basic analytical tool for determining which processes deserve the most attention and investment.

Process mapping - A method of graphically displaying the key factors in how processes are organized in an enterprise. (Source: Daly and Freeman, *Road to Excellence*)

Process owner (Also known as **Process team leader**) - The individual responsible for coordinating the long-term vision and migration plan for each process. The process owner is also responsible for creating quantum leaps for processes, advocating/maintaining enterprise process focus, and linking with continuous process improvement. (Source: Daly and Freeman, *Road to Excellence*)

Process paradox - Occurs when organizations experience little or no (or even negative) improvement while they were making dramatic improvements to their processes by focusing improvement efforts on processes that do not substantially affect the capabilities that create value, and value creation. (Source: Peter Keen, *Process Edge*)

Process team - A cross-functional team responsible for periodic monitoring of a process for continuous improvement, designing, developing and recommending process improvements, conducting root cause analysis, maintaining and updating process documentation, and linking sub-process performance to process performance. (Source: Daly and Freeman, *Road to Excellence*)

Profile - Sets the context for the way your organization operates. Your environment, key working relationships, initiatives underway, key processes, and strategic challenges serve as an overarching guide for your organization's progress on implementing Process Based Management. (Source: NIST Baldrige Award Criteria)

QS Standards - A set of standards relating to quality assurance and quality management.

Quality function deployment - A process that ensures that customer requirements are accurately translated into relevant technical requirements, prioritized with the aid of competitive data, through each stage of the product or service development cycle.

Reengineering - Radical redesign of business processes for dramatic improvement (as opposed to the incremental improvement associated with continuous improvement efforts). (Source: Michael Hammer, *Beyond Reengineering*)

Scenario planning - A scenario is an internally consistent (shared and agreed upon) view of what the future might turn out to be. By constructing multiple scenarios, an organization can systematically explore the possible consequences of uncertainty for its choice of strategies. (Source: Michael Porter, *Competitive Advantage*)

SCM – Supply Chain Management - Supply-chain management includes managing supply and demand, sourcing raw materials and parts, manufacturing and assembly, warehousing and inventory tracking, order entry and order management, distribution across all channels, and delivery to the customer. (Source: Supply Chain.org)

Simulation - The technique of observing and manipulating an artificial mechanism (model) that represents a real-world process, which, for technical or economic reasons, is not suitable or available for direct experimentation. (Source: Gabriel Pall, *Process Centered Enterprise*)

Six Sigma - 1. Level of process performance equivalent to producing only 1.4 defects for every one million opportunities or operations.
2. Term used to describe Process Improvement initiatives using sigma-based process measures and/or striving for Six Sigma level performance.

Stakeholder - Those who have an interest (a stake) in the organization and set the boundaries for an organization. Stakeholders consist of: shareholders, customers, employees, creditors, suppliers and community members.

Target costing - A target cost is calculated by subtracting a desired profit from an estimated or a market-based price to arrive at a desired production, engineering, or marketing cost. This may not be the initial production cost, but one expected to be achieved during the mature production stage. A method used in the analysis of product and process design that involves estimating a target cost and designing a product to meet that cost. (Source: CAM-I Glossary)

Time-based management - Using time as a strategic weapon by identifying market opportunities and responding to those opportunities before competitors; responding to customers' needs in their own time frame; and eliminating non-value-added activities. (Source: Society of Management Accountants of Canada, *Time-based Management*)

TL 9000 - A series of standards relating to quality assurance and quality management in the Telecommunications Sector, fashioned after ISO 9000.

Tool - Anything used as a means of accomplishing a task or purpose:

TQM - Term used to describe broad implementation of quality management company-wide; a customer focused, unifying management approach encompassing every aspect of an organizations operations. (Source: Gabriel Pall, *Process Centered Enterprise*)

Value chain - The linked set of value creating activities all the way from basic raw material sources, through to component suppliers, to the ultimate end-use product delivered into the final consumer's hand, and in today's world, perhaps recycling to the beginning of a new value chain cycle. (Source: Shank and Govindarajan, *Strategic Cost Management*)

Value-added activity - An activity or process that is judged to contribute to customer value or satisfy an organizational need. The attribute "value-added" reflects a belief that the activity or process cannot be eliminated without reducing the quantity, responsiveness, or quality of output required by a customer or organization. (Source: CAM-I Glossary)

Voice of the customer - A customer value monitoring process that strives to understand the drivers of customer satisfaction. Customer needs drive processes. (Source: Daly and Freeman, *Road to Excellence*)

White space - The space between the boxes on an organization chart. The space created by concentrating on the flow of products, paper and information *within* departments or functions rather than the flows *between* departments or functions. (Source: Rummler and Brache, *Improving Performance: How to Manage the White Space on the Organization Chart*)

Work in the process - The day-to-day activities involved in executing an organization's processes.

Work on the process - Proactive actions to improve the efficiency and effectiveness of processes.

APPENDIX B:

EXECUTIVE SUMMARY
CAM-I Case Studies In Process Management

BELL CANADA
NETWORK OPERATIONS

Introduction

Bell Canada is a wholly owned subsidiary of BCE (Bell Canada Enterprises) and is Canada's largest supplier of telecommunication services. In early 1994, Bell Canada found itself in a major shift in the competitive marketplace. The emergence of new technologies along with the introduction of new competitors placed significant pressure on Bell Canada's existing cost structure. In response to these external environmental forces, Bell Canada established a cost reduction target to reduce operating expenses by 30%. Although Bell Canada was able to obtain the cost reduction target, the implementation of the "less costly" operating plan resulted in hindered customer service levels.

Along the way to achieving the cost reduction targets, a group within Bell Canada realized that there was a better way - process management. This group, Network Services, believed that using the tools of process management would improve the cost structure of the organization in such a way that would result in better processes used to deliver value to their customers.

Case Study Evaluation

Strategy Formulation: The strategy articulated by Bell Canada's President and senior management team, although well communicated, did not link the business transformation efforts specifically to process management. As a result the process of the business transformation included aspects of process management; however these efforts were disjointed.

Process Clarity: Primary and support business processes were defined as part of the Business Transformation Project; however, the process definitions were not communicated widely. This resulted in a lack of end-to-end process awareness at the performer level. In addition, although process owners were named, functional managers were still empowered to manage customer service and run the day-to-day operations. Thus the Business Transformation Project focused on individual functional silo improvement initiatives. Absent the proper linkage of the end-to-end process across functional silos, customer service suffered.

Process Awareness: Process awareness was developed throughout Network Service via communication sessions using a newly created process management infrastructure. Process measures and performance management agreements were created to help job performers understand respective responsibilities throughout the process; however action was never taken on the results of the performance measures. Thus although Bell Canada was successful in establishing employee willingness to accept change, they did not create an environment were performers could clearly relate to their process or the associated process measures.

Process Ownership and Control: Process owners were appointed in Network Services, but process owners were not given the authority to make end-to-end changes. To succeed, Bell Canada will need to enhance process awareness, empower process owners to make changes in the end-to-end processes, and establish process accountability and responsibility by linking compensation to process based performance criteria.

Migration to a Process-Centered Organization: Network Services is clearly migrating to Process Based Management. The migration to process management has been led by Network Operations and is focused towards a balanced approach that includes quality, cost and time performance

improvements. To be successful throughout the entire
organization, the process management initiative will need a
more complete process management process including a
cross functional steering team responsible for developing,
training, integrating and implementing process
management.

Performance Measures: A new measurement system is
being put into place. Bell Canada is shifting to a
measurement system that has a market-customer focus and a
process driven structure. Bell Canada has a good
understanding of the importance of "white space measures"
to support the appropriate customer focus of performance
measurement. However, not all measures have clear owners
and compensation is not tied to process results. It appears
that this is due to the performance measures being more
mature than the process being measured. The measurement
development system needs to slow down and focus needs to
shift to establishing better process clarity and ownership.

Continuous Improvement: Bell Canada has used many
different improvement tools during the business
transformation initiative, however it has been a challenge to
get all the various initiatives linked together using these
tools. Process improvement opportunities are being
identified through brainstorming sessions and the use of
"as-is" mapping. Customer service level agreements and
feedback acquired through surveys, face-to-face meetings
and telephone contacts enable the process teams to
understand the customer. The process owner and the

process teams establish process goals and performance measures. However, there is no framework for dialogue around process improvement. Although good plans are developed and checked, they are often not acted upon. Processes must be managed by process owners and evaluated on process goals that are tied to strategy.

Toolset: This area of process management is not an issue for Bell Canada. The toolset employed consisted of RBG Methodology, Memory Jogger Plus, Visio, Excel, Optima, and Survey Tracker. The standard set of tools enabled the facilitators to focus on results achieved by using the tools, instead of the tools themselves. Bell Canada intends to find a process simulation tool to assist process teams.

Overall Conclusion

Bell Canada has started the journey to Process Based Management and Network Services is well on its way to success. While the initial movement towards business transformation through cost reduction efforts resulted in negatively impacted customer service, the process of change introduced the concept and importance of improving service delivery by focusing on the customer.

To be successful at Bell Canada, the process management initiative will need greater focus with a commitment to developing a cohesive process to coordinate and align all the various improvement initiatives. Process management is a powerful tool to guide and measure an organization towards achieving its long term objectives; however, process management requires a long term organizational commitment and a focused, well orchestrated approach to make it work.

EXECUTIVE SUMMARY
CAM-I Case Studies in Process Management

UNITED STATES MARINE CORPS
BUSINESS ENTERPRISE

Introduction

The Corps introduction to business process reengineering began in 1992 as part of the quest for a better database method to track combat development and implementation actions. Using activity-based costing, the USMC discovered that within the Business Enterprise, they spent as much as 90% of its resources on internal negotiations. The business enterprise was sub-optimizing its most valuable internal resource - its people. Emboldened by the discovery of its internal "flaws," the Corps launched an effort to identify the "to-be" enterprise and to reorganize and optimize the reengineered business processes.

Case Study Evaluation

Strategy Formulation: The Corps identified the "to-be" business enterprise and developed a strategy to optimize their core business processes.   The senior leadership embedded process management in its mission, vision, strategies and goals and communicated this vision to the entire Corps. Senior leaders still need to clearly articulate the distinction between the role of process and functional ownership and establish a process for process management.

Process Clarity: The USMC Business Enterprise has a complete map of processes portrayed as the "Galactic Radiator" showing key activities and core business processes. They need to develope a clear set of specific future process objectives, including any explicit training and education efforts for attaining greater process clarity.

Process Awareness: There is a broad understanding and acceptance of process management at the Headquarters level which is reinforced through communication and training sessions. More people need to get involved, especially at the general officer level. The general officers do not view process management as distinct from their functional roles nor as a priority. Process awareness efforts at this level need to be reenergized.

Process Ownership and Control: The Corps developed a visual icon called the "galactic radiator," that arrays functional leadership vertically against process ownership horizontally in a management matrix. Roles and responsibilities are clearly defined, however, eemployees at all levels are not involved. Employee involvement is the key to making change effective. The Corps needs to renew the process management focus at the general officer level, establish permanent process teams and a chain of accountability.

Performance Measures: The Strategic Plan for the Business Enterprise repeatedly emphasizes the importance and need for performance measures. The Corps has a strategy in place and articulated performance criteria, but has not internalized how the measures should be used. The measures do not influence behavior, but do influence how processes are developed. "If you don't measure it, you can't manage it" is realized but not implemented. The Corps needs to develop an effective strategy for internalizing the use of performance measures.

Migration to a Process-Centered Organization: The Marine Corps is making some progress in its migration to Process Based Management. The Corps articulated its processes and management teams in its master plan along with a unified operational process strategy linked effectively to the budget. The commitment to migration is most clearly demonstrated in the Marine Corps Order for the Total Force Structure process and the initial definition of working relationships between processes and functional organizations. However, there is no further evidence that the migration plan was communicated, adopted or implemented beyond these initial areas. The Corps needs to refocus and reenergize the process owners on the process management strategy and adopt a consistent migration approach (including process performance measures) to implement that strategy.

Continuous Improvement: The current continuous improvement efforts are very strong and follow a solid history of initiatives, starting with Total Quality Leadership. Process improvement efforts are an integral part of the overall strategy and are defined in the Business Enterprise Strategic Plan. Process management teams are planning and in some cases using customer surveys, focus groups, ABC, process modeling, simulation, data modeling and benchmarking to develop improvement goals. These goals are communicated across the organization by process owners/teams, the Marine Corps Continuous Process Improvement Program Director, "missionaries", newsletters, video presentations, press coverage and the Web site. The missing link in this environment is a process performance measurement system and a reporting system to monitor and communicate process performance, linking improvement results to the reward and performance system. This is "the" stumbling block to continuous improvement initiatives.

Overall Conclusion

The Marine Corps is making progress on its journey to a Process Based Management organization. It is approaching a process maturity level where core processes are integrated;

however, a potential impediment to a holistic, optimal organization is the lack of maturity in performance measures.

The challenges facing the Marine Corps are to more fully communicate and execute the vision and strategy and to develop a process based management performance evaluation system.

EXECUTIVE SUMMARY
CAM-I Case Studies in Process Management

STATOIL

Introduction

StatOil is the world's third-largest net seller of crude oil and a substantial supplier of natural gas in Europe, with subsidiaries in 23 countries including the U.S.A. In 2000, the Norwegian state-owned company faced intensified competition in the oil industry, low profitability relative to its competitors and considerable opportunities for growth. These challenges drove the desire to improve efficiency and profitability, with a targeted increase from 4.7 percent to 10 percent ROCE, through performance-based management and control.

The organization's initial move toward Process Based Management began in 1995 when it recognized that a common IT solution was needed. The resulting strategy was to change the organization structure, change processes and adopt a common IT strategy. Several organizational changes were made, a business process reengineering project was embarked on, and SAP was adopted as the corporate-wide IT solution. The team responsible for implementing SAP identified that a process-based orientation was critical for success and, while middle management resisted such, the Board supported a process approach. While the driver for the strategic change was IT improvement, the orientation for implementing much of the strategy was based on business processes.

Case Study Evaluation

Strategy Formulation: While some senior managers understand the benefits of a process orientation, there is no corporate-level vision, strategy or support for Process Based Management. StatOil's corporate strategy is driven by its unsatisfactory earnings over the 1996-1998 periods. Although select downstream processes appear to have a strong process management orientation, corporate management is focused on upstream operations. Further, the downstream process efforts are compromised by frequent organizational changes and conflicting national priorities. Overall, neither StatOil's vision or strategy incorporate process-based thinking, nor the limited successes experienced so far are in jeopardy of being reversed as the organization is largely returning to its previous functional & geographic structure.

Process Clarity: Some significant efforts to advance process understanding have been taken, but they were largely restricted in scope and often limited in duration. One organizational group, the Nordic Process Centre, was established to be responsible for optimization of processes and connections between organizations & processes. As part of the reengineering project, StatOil's seven primary processes were clearly defined, documented, and widely communicated at numerous information meetings. Process owners were established for each process, but their roles have not been developed. While most front-line workers have a clear understanding of their processes, process documentation is rarely used. Processes have not been defined beyond the highest level, and existing process documentation does not always reflect changes made to these processes. StatOil must advance a process vision beyond initial high-level efforts with the seven primary processes. This will require significant additional process definition, documentation, communication, training and establishing process ownership roles.

Process Awareness: Process awareness is not embedded in the organization. Understanding of process structure was initially developed and communicated through informal meetings among a group of high-potential employees given responsibility for a change to process orientation, and the workers, lower and middle managers in each process. However, the group coordinating this effort was disbanded after a brief existence, and process understanding never became widespread. Job descriptions do not reflect process roles, communications with employees do not reference processes, process owner roles remain undefined, and there is little distinction between process and function throughout the company. Beyond a few senior managers and the members of the Nordic Process Centre, there is little understanding of the elements of process management or the process-related efforts StatOil has already performed. Overall, the lack of a process for advancing process management and the training required for such are the company's key shortcomings in instilling process awareness.

Process Ownership and Control: Process ownership is in a very primitive stage. Few process managers or owners exist, there are no established roles or training for the position, and although it is recognized that process ownership is essential for success, there is no plan to expand the ownership concept. Further, there is no forum in which current process owners meet, and no informal communication mechanisms exist in lieu of such. There is an explicit understanding that a process orientation is only beginning and is at a critical stage, yet senior management has not formed a strategy to move the process initiative forward.

Performance Measures: The Company's approach to performance measurement is relatively robust, but the process-based and leading-indicator orientation remains underdeveloped. A portfolio of financial, quality, customer satisfaction and some process-based performance measures have been created, as has a system to report on them. The recently-developed process-related measures are the most limited in scope and least mature in development.

Measurement data is routinely reported and are used in assessing performance. Measurement reports are provided to and acted on at both high and low organizational levels. StatOil will not have a truly balanced measurement portfolio until some leading indicators are developed which gauge innovation and learning & growth issues, and additional aspects of quality and customer satisfaction are incorporated In addition, the company has not made any progress in linking rewards to performance measurement results. Overall, further developing measures of process performance and enhancing their significance and usage is a key requirement for progressing toward process management.

Migration to a Process-Centered Organization: In many regards, StatOil is ready to migrate to Process Based Management, and change has become part of the StatOil culture. However, no process has been developed to manage such a shift, and no mandate exists for making a shift. There is substantial process knowledge, skills and desire for migration within the Nordic Process Centre; expanding this throughout the organization is critical to moving forward. Establishing process training, owners, teams, a process for migration and acquiring active executive sponsorship are required.

Continuous Improvement: Continuous improvement and employee empowerment are essential elements of StatOil's basic values. Although no explicit continuous improvement program exists, and employees are not given dedicated time to work on improvement projects, employees feel it is part of their job. They are supported by a system which captures problems (mainly claims) and a set of specific criteria applied in the problem solving process. A required emphasis is moving process workers from a problem-solving orientation focused on discrete steps of the process to a holistic systems-based approach of overall process improvement. As many of the efforts required to advance process management, for continuous improvement to evolve will require additional resources for process training, tools, more and updated process documentation and time to address process improvement.

Toolset: A standard tool is used to document processes, another tool is used to control process change requests, and the ERP system is used to guide the implementation of processes. Other tools that are useful in advancing process management are absent, including those, which support cost management, voice of the customer, quality management, operations planning and strategic planning. Once a significant, broad shift to a process orientation mindset occurs, particularly at the executive ranks, tools will be an important augmentation to a variety of implementation efforts.

Overall Conclusion

StatOil is in the early stages of the journey to Process Based Management. Steps have been taken on several fronts to advance a process orientation. The Nordic Process Centre in many regards represents a "center of process excellence." The knowledge and passion of existing process managers and many process performers is the key component of process migration. StatOil's primary challenges are to engage executive management in understanding and sponsoring Process Based Management, develop a process for designing and implementing it, and to receive adequate resources to make process management happen.

EXECUTIVE SUMMARY
CAM-I Case Studies in Process Management

USAF/BOEING
SUPPLY CHAIN PROCESS MANAGEMENT

Introduction

During the 1990's the United States Air Force entered into a partnership with Boeing Aerospace to implement joint supply chain management across the two cross-functional organizations. The USAF was represented in this effort by its Aeronautical Systems Center Commercial Aircraft Integrated Product Team (CA-IPT) whose mission includes using innovative acquisition practices to acquire and support commercial aircraft systems. Boeing was represented by its Derivative Airplanes Division (DAP) established in response to a Secretary of Defense mandate to use nongovernmental specifications for nonmilitary airplanes purchased by the government. The mandate was seen as an opportunity for Boeing to sell 747's to the government.

The two organizations, acting as a supply team, crafted a strategy to create a joint supply chain process called "an integrated fleet" ("pseudo airline") whereby all Boeing airplanes in the USAF fleet were under the same support umbrella. The challenge to implementing the desired changes is evident in the contrasts between the military and commercial sector. Differences existed in acquisition, supply, requirement definitions, implementation, statutory requirements, etc. The supply team adopted a process based management structure to overcome those differences, improve efficiency and quality; train people better and have a positive impact on customer satisfaction. The process based management structure links core competencies and core processes together with specific goals linked to measures.

Case Study Evaluation

Strategy Formulation: The USAF Single Program Director and the Boeing Program Manager jointly set the strategic direction of the effort. Process Based Management is recognized as the key to success. The IPT and DAP teams work individually to secure buy in from their organizations. Process Based Management at Boeing is clearly articulated and linked to corporate strategy and core competencies. The Air Force needs to obtain senior leadership commitment to be able to succeed in implementing the Process Based Management initiative.

Process Clarity: A centralized database to house the process documentation was created.   While some process documentation exists, there needs to be agreement on the definition of the supply chain processes and how they link to USAF and Boeing processes.   Further, core processes, measures and process boundaries must be defined. Documented processes should be used in the development of employee training programs.

Process Awareness: There is broad understanding of processes by top managers and some employees are beginning to describe their jobs in term of process, but no training program exists for the implementation of Process Based Management.   Process understanding must expand from understanding of organizational processes to understanding of roles within the supply chain processes. Both organizations have tailored existing processes to the new environment and some job descriptions include process responsibilities.   Process responsibilities need to be included in all performance development plans.

Process Ownership and Control: Process Based Management is clearly the focus of the unit.   Supply chain processes are developed jointly by IPT and DAP.   The importance of defining process roles and responsibilities and tying them to metrics is understood.   When developing processes, owner roles and responsibilities must be detailed, team responsibilities defined, measures put in place, and training provided.

Performance Measures: The IPT and DAP team are developing process performance measures and linking them to strategy. Metrics must be developed and owners defined at the time the process is defined. Measures must be tied to compensation and linked across processes.

Migration to a Process-Centered Organization: Processes are being deployed to support the goals and objectives of the strategic and operating plans. They are beginning to incorporate incentive clauses in contracts based on process improvement and cost savings.   Process documentation, roles, measures and ties to compensation, currently under development, must be completed.

Continuous Improvement: The overall strategy and team structure supports continuous improvement. The available systems for communicating process information serve to inform and educate employees. The IPT and DAP teams improve processes based on program experience and continue to come up with new ways of doing business. The continuous improvement effort must evolve to be proactive versus reactive. Improvement goals must be established and follow a coordinated approach. Achieving the continuous improvement goals continues to be hampered by the lack of comprehensive process measures.

Overall Conclusion

The USAF/Boeing partnership has made progress on the "Road to Excellence". The joint IPT/DAP approach enables the organizations to leverage respective strengths to overcome challenges. Significant progress will be achieved when clear goals are defined. Then, all supply chain processes can be defined, measures established and the roles and responsibilities of the process performers and owners identified.

Both organizations realize the journey in becoming a process-based organization is slow and time consuming. An unwavering commitment by both organizations is required to sustain the momentum of the implementation effort. One step in the right direction involves a mindset shift to viewing this effort as a process, not a project.

EXECUTIVE SUMMARY CAM-I Case Studies in Process Management

SANTEE COOPER

Introduction

Santee Cooper, formally known as the South Carolina Public Service Authority, is a state-owned non-profit organization established in 1934. Santee Cooper is the third largest public power utility in the United States. The primary product is electricity.

Santee Cooper began to focus on the importance and relevance of Process Based Management during the 1995-96 strategic planning process. At that time, the possibility of becoming de-regulated led them to strive to be a low cost, low price generator and provider of electricity. The overriding organizational focus is on remaining the lowest-priced provider of electricity. Santee Cooper has identified the three key requirements for electric service as low price, high reliability, and satisfactory customer service.

Case Study Evaluation

Strategy Formulation: The CEO and executive and senior-vice presidents create and revise the corporate strategic plan. Annually, the CEO personally communicates strategic direction. The overwhelming organizational focus is on providing low-priced power and keeping customers satisfied. The majority of management focus is on continual cost reduction.

An ABM Evolution Plan was developed to define the initial action plans to introduce process thinking. Senior management bought into ABM Evolution Plan development, but not into its implementation. The lack of senior support and formal ownership prevents the ABM Evolution Plan from moving forward.

Process Clarity: Santee Cooper uses an Oracle financial-based information system to capture financial activity. Within the Financial Information System (FIS), projects and tasks are linked to value chain activities. The corporate value chain clearly identifies the core and support processes.

There is no formally accepted method for defining processes other than in the value chain. Since senior management has not brought the value chain to the forefront, there is little attention paid to processes. As a result there is no formal mechanism in place for individuals to understand how they create value for their customers.

Process Awareness: Santee Cooper has a solid project management program with project team roles evolving as part of the culture. Cross-functional teams, committees and projects are established on an "as needed" basis. Project teams have some process structure, but they focus on projects rather than processes. Process advocates exist at multiple levels of the organization.

When processes are changed by projects, there is no clear communication or capture of process changes and results. Most importantly, process awareness tools (ABM Evolution Plan, value chain, balanced scorecard) are in place and need to be implemented corporate-wide. There is little or no process awareness at Santee Cooper except for the process advocates and a few employees involved in IT and supply chain projects. Job description roles and responsibilities are functionally based.

Process Ownership and Control: Process ownership is at the formation stage. Few process teams exist and there are no defined roles and responsibilities. Santee Cooper has no formal process structure for the selection of teams and owners. Processes are mainly sustained through managing process inputs and outputs.

Performance Measures: The ABM Evolution Plan, balanced scorecards, and the value chain all provide the foundation for developing a process performance measurement system. These tools are the drivers for developing process performance measures. The Corporate

Goals Incentive Program attempts to link individual and department goals to corporate strategy. However, the focus remains on reducing costs, not managing costs.

There are too many measures in use. It is not clear that the current measures are the right ones. Most performance measures do not relate to outcomes and processes.

Migration to a Process-Centered Organization: A discontinued Program for Employee Participation (PEP) planted the seeds for culture change by improving communications and facilitating change. PEP trained facilitators are now in some key managerial positions. Most of the essential ingredients to migrate to a Process Based Management organization are in place (ABM Evolution Plan, value chain, balanced scorecard).

The process management migration effort could be centered on the ABM Evolution Plan and the value chain, but the plan has not been implemented since it has little support from, and has not been communicated beyond, senior management. As a result of lack of management buy-in, there is no formal plan as to how Santee Cooper will migrate to process based management. Internally, there are no formal tools to facilitate the sharing of best practices.

Continuous Improvement: All levels of employees, from front-line to executive management, can initiate improvement efforts. There is no formal continuous improvement program and continuous improvement efforts are not explicitly part of Santee Cooper's overall strategy. Project prioritization is not tied to strategy. Most efforts are project-based and seek to improve a specific process or functional subset thereof. There is no organization-wide process to capture or share improvement learning's. However, Operations has developed a standard format for capturing and tracking improvement efforts.

Overall Conclusion

Santee Cooper is poised to become a Process Based Management organization. The foundation for this initiative is already in place. The Goals Team developed a detailed and comprehensive ABM Evolution Plan; the organization then failed to implement it. The plan also provides the tools (including balanced scorecards, corporate value chain, FIS, and ABC/M). In addition, Santee Cooper had implemented and then abandoned the PEP program that trained facilitators and taught management skills, problem identification, problem resolution and communication skills.

APPENDIX C:

Process Management Bibliography since Road to Excellence

Resources Specifically Related to Process Management (Must Read):

CAM-I Cost Management Integration Team, *Value Quest: Driving Profit and Performance by Integrating a Strategic Management Processes,* CAM-I, Bedford, TX, 2000.

CAM-I Process Management Interest Group, *CAM-I Case Studies in Process Management: Bell Canada,* CAM-I, Bedford, TX, December, 1998.

CAM-I Process Management Interest Group, *CAM-I Case Studies in Process Management: Statoil,* CAM-I, Bedford, TX, September, 2000.

CAM-I Process Management Interest Group, *CAM-I Case Studies in Process Management: United States Air Force/Boeing Supply Chain Process,* CAM-I, Bedford, TX, December, 2001.

CAM-I Process Management Interest Group, *CAM-I Case Studies in Process Management: United States Marine Corps Business Enterprise*, CAM-I, Bedford, TX, May, 1999.

Dowdle, Pat, Stevens, Jerry, McCarty, Bob and Dennis Daly," Process-Based Management: The Road to Excellence," *Cost Management*, July/August, 2003, pages 12-19.

Dye, R.W., "The World of Work in 2010," *CMA Management*, December/January, 2002, pages 38-41.

Freeman, Tom; Daly, Dennis; Dowdle, Pat and Jerry Stevens, "Measuring and Managing Process Performance: Key Issues and Recommendations," *International Journal of Agile Manufacturing*, Vol. 4, Issue 1, 2001, pages 97-106.

Gardner, Robert A., "Resolving The Process Paradox: A Strategy for launching meaningful process improvement," *Quality Progress*, March 2001, pages 51-59.

Gardner, Robert A., *The Process-Focused Organization: A Transition Strategy for Success*, Milwaukee, WI, American Society for Quality, 2004.

Garvin, David, "Leveraging Processes for Strategic Advantage: Roundtable with Xerox's Allaire, USAA's Herres, Smithkline Beecham's Leschly, and Pepsi's Weatherup," *Harvard Business Review*, September/October, 1995, Volume 73, Number 5, pages 76-90.

Hammer, Michael, *The Agenda: What Every Business Must Do to Dominate the Decade*, New York, NY, Crown Business, 2001, Chapter 4.

Keen, Peter G.W., *The Process Edge: Creating Value Where It Counts*, Boston, MA, Harvard Business School Press, 1997. Chapters 1-3

Leahy, Tad, "The Ultimate Initiative," *Business Finance*, November, 1999, pages 57-59.

Matchrzak, Ann and Qianwei Wang, "Breaking the Functional Mind-set in Process Organizations," *Harvard Business Review*, September/October, 1996, Volume 74, Number 5, pages 92-99.

McCormack, Kevin and Bill Johnson, "Business Process Orientation, Supply Chain Management, and the e-corporation," *IIE Solutions*, October, 2001, pages 33-37.

Spanyi, Andrew, *Business Process Management Is A Team Sport: Play To Win*, Tampa, FL., Anclote Press, 2003.

Society of Management Accountants of Canada, *"Implementing Process Management: A Framework for Action,"* Management Accounting Guideline #47, CMA Canada, Hamilton, Ont., October, 1998.

Resources with Limited Process Management Relevancy:

Brache, Alan P., *How Organizations Work: Taking a Holistic Approach to Enterprise Health*, New York, NY: John Wiley and Sons, Inc., 2002.

Brimson, James, *Handbook of Process- Based Accounting: Leveraging Processes to Predict Results*, New York, NY, AICPA, 2002.

CAM-I Service Process Interest Group, *Service Process Measurement: Breaking the Code*, Bedford, TX: CAM-I, August 1998.

Carr, Nicholas, "A New Way to Manage Process Knowledge," *Harvard Business Review*, September/October, 1999, Volume 77, Number 5, pages 24-25.

Foti, Ross, "Maturity," *PM Network*, September, 2002, pages 39-43.

Gardner, Robert, "Resolving the Process Paradox," *Quality Progress*, March, 2001, pages 51-59.

Hammer, Michael and Steven Stanton, "How Process Enterprises Really Work," *Harvard Business Review*, November/December, 1999, Volume 77, Number 6, pages 108-118.

Hammer, Michael, "Process Management and the Future of Six Sigma," *Sloan Management Review*, Winter 2002, pages 26-32.

Harmon, Paul (Editor), "Business Process Architecture and the Process-Centric Company," *Business Process Trends*, March, 2003, Volume 1, No.3, pages 1-11.

Humphrey, Watts S. *Managing the Software Process*, Reading, MA, Addison-Wesley, 1990.

Institute of Management Accountants, Arthur Andersen LLP, and CAM-I, *"Implementing Process Management for Improving Products and Services,"* Statement on Management Accounting#4NN, Montvale, NJ, April, 2000.

Jackson, Harry K. Jr. and Normand L. Frigon, *Management 2000: The Practical Guide to World Class Competition*. New York, NY: Van Nostrand Reinhold, 1994. Chapter 5.

Leahy, Tad, "ABM on Steroids," *Business Finance*, September, 2001, pages 46-48.

Lofts, Norman, *Process Visualization: An Executive Guide to Business Process Design*, Etobicoke, Ontario, Canada: John Wiley and Sons, Inc. 2002.

McCormack, Kevin, "Business Process Orientation: Do You Have It?" *Quality Progress*, January, 2001, pages 51-57.

Pall, Gabriel A. *The Process-Centered Enterprise: The Power of Commitments*, Boca Raton, FL, St. Lucie Press, 2000.

Sharman, Paul, "Activity/Process Budgets: A Tool for Change Management," *CMA: The Management Accounting Magazine*, March, 1996, Volume 70, Issue 2, pages 21-24

Society of Management Accountants of Canada, *"Implementing Business Process Redesign,"* Management Accounting Guideline #21, Hamilton, Ont., CMA Canada, December, 1993.

Society of Management Accountants of Canada, *"Next Generation Enterprise,* Emerging Issues Paper, Mississauga, Ontario, Canada, 2000.

Resources Environmentally Related to Process Management:

Epstein, Marc and Bill Birchard, *Counting What Counts: Turning Corporate Accountability to Competitive Advantage*, Reading, MA., 1999.

Hamel, Gary, "Strategy as Revolution," *Harvard Business Review*, July/August, 1996, pages 69-82.

Hiebeler, R., Kelly, T. and C. Ketteman, *Best Practices: Building Your Business with Customer-Focused Solutions*, New York, NY, Arthur Andersen/Simon and Schuster, 1999.

Hope, Jeremy and Tony Hope, *Competing in the Third Wave: The Ten Key Management Issues of the Information Age*, Boston, MA., Harvard Business School Press, 1997. Issue #4.

Johnson, H. Thomas and Anders Broms, *Profit Beyond Measure*, New York, Free Press, 2000.

Kaplan, Robert and Robin Cooper, *Cost and Effect: Using Integrated Cost Systems to Drive Profitability and Performance*, Boston, MA., Harvard Business School Press, 1998.

Kaplan, Robert and David Norton, *The Balanced Scorecard*, Boston, MA, Harvard Business School Press, 1996.

Macdonald, John, *Calling A Halt to Mindless Change: A Plea for Commonsense Management*, New York, NY, AMACOM, 1998.

Mintzberg, Henry, "Reflecting on the Strategy Process," *Sloan Management Review,* Spring 1999, pages 21-30.

Moore, Geoffrey A., *Crossing the Chasm,* New York, NY, HarperBusiness, 1991.

Ostroff, Frank, *The Horizontal Organization: What the Organization of the Future Looks Like and Howe It Delivers Value to Customers,* New York, NY, Oxford University Press, 1999. Chapters 1, 3, 11, 12

Pasternack, Bruce and Albert Viscio, *The Centerless Corporation: A New Model for Transforming Your Organization for Growth and Prosperity,* New York, NY, Simon and Schuster, 1999.

Shank, John and Vijay Govindarajan, *Strategic Cost Management: The New Tool for Competitive Advantage,* New York, NY, Free Press, 1993.

Society of Management Accountants of Canada, *"Applying the Balanced Scorecard,"* Management Accounting Guideline: Strategic Management Series, Hamilton, Ont, January, 2000.

INDEX

MANY OTHER PUBLICATIONS
ARE AVAILABLE FROM THE
CAM-I LIBRARY

For information about other CAM-I publications,
or to receive a copy of the most current
CAM-I Library Catalog, contact:

CAM-I Library Services

Telephone 817/426/5744

FAX 817/426/5799

E-mail: nancyt@cam-i.org

http://www.cam-i.org/storeindex.cfm

VALUE QUEST: DRIVING PROFIT & PERFORMANCE BY INTEGRATING STRATEGIC MANAGEMENT PROCESSES

The CAM-I Cost Management Integration Team & C.J. McNair

With the introduction of the CAM-I Strategic Process Model, Value Quest provides practitioners a powerful framework to convert key information flows into optimal organizational strategies and executable decisions. Placed within the Extended Enterprise Concept, the CAM-I Strategic Management Process Model outlines the dynamic information flows between seven critical Strategic Management Processes (SMPs) and demonstrates the exponential "power" of leveraged information and systemic thinking.

Value Quest introduces the Decision Domain Hierarchy, a refined decision categorization, facilitating the visibility of a firm's key decisions and information requirements. Value Quest furnishes the reader with comprehensive explanations of seven Strategic Management Processes (SMPs), graphically displaying their information requirements and demonstrating the competitive force gained through CAM-I's Integration Model:

* Target Cost Management
* Activity-Based Cost Management
* Integrated Performance Management
* Asset Management
* Process Management
* Capacity Management
* Extended Enterprise

Outfitted with a Diagnostic Positioning Tool (disk included), Value Quest answers the "Why's" and "How's" of Strategic Management Process Integration. With the compilation of fourteen years of leading-edge research, the CAM-I CMS Program again sets the industry standard for quantum improvement.

Price--$39.95

ABC PRIMER

Authors: Gary Cokins, Alan Stratton & Jack Helbling

This document, written with a clear, informed understanding of what ABC is all about, is based on real implementation experiences. The "Three R's" now revitalizing the way business is conducted in the United States are Reengineering, Reinventing, and Redesigning processes. Traditionally, accounting systems are not designed to deliver managerial information. Activity Based information significantly boosts the value and utility of financial data for decision-makers and empowered employees. This primer addresses the lack of awareness of what ABC is and is not. It is not written as a "how to implement" cookbook, but does give a head start for action.

Price--$14.95

TARGET COSTING: THE NEXT FRONTIER IN STRATEGIC COST MANAGEMENT

Authors: The CAM-I Target Cost Core Group & Profs Shahid Ansari & Jan Bell

This book provides practical insights on how to use target costing for profit planning and cost management. The purpose is to show that target costing is a management method that allows firms to provide customers with products that they want, when they want them, at a price they can afford, and still earn adequate financial returns.

The book extends the existing knowledge base by focusing on the details of how target costing works in practice. The authors relied on state-of-the-art practices drawn from translations of papers available only in the Japanese language and the collective experience of several world class companies: Arthur Andersen LLP, The Boeing Company, Chrysler Corporation, Eastman Kodak Company and Texas Instruments.

Materials in this book are not currently available in the English language business literature. Practicing managers will find that this document contains a balance between general concepts and technical information required for their application. Examples from industry are used to illustrate important issues and current practice.

Key topics in the book include:
1. How target costing relates to business strategy and profit planning
2. A process model that links target costing with the product development cycle
3. The linkages between customer requirements and costing
4. Tools, information and measurement systems required to support target costing

Price--$44.95

THE ROAD TO EXCELLENCE: BECOMING A PROCESS-BASED COMPANY

Authors: The CAM-I Process Management Interest Group Revised and Edited by Dennis Daly and Tom Freeman

The goal of this book is to understand the importance of process management in planning and achieving the objectives of the corporation. The authors are process strategists, implementers and practitioners from various manufacturing and service companies, consulting firms, and universities who wish to share their experiences and insights on the advantages of becoming a process-centered company and on the considerations that should be made in migrating from a functional to a process-focused organization. The book is organized into four sections:

Section 1 - Creates the strategic vision for process management; clarifies the hierarchy and the concept of core process development; provides suggestions for introducing process management within the organization and addresses organizational and behavioral issues; and defines the roles and responsibilities of process owners, controllers and performers.

Section 2 - Provides guidance on migrating from a functionally-focused to a process-focused organization using a 4-step program to assess, develop, implement and embed process management within an organization.

Section 3- Introduces the concepts of sustaining process management through analyzing current and future-state processes in relationship to customers and markets; develops activity and process metrics relating value, time, quality, flexibility and functionality to maintain customer focus; and provides guidance for using continuous process improvement in strategic, tactical and operational planning and performance.

Section 4 - Conclusions and summary. The book is intended for business publication readers with emphasis on companies of all sizes that are exploring, planning and implementing process management in their organizations. The Road To Excellence applies both to service and manufacturing firms and target readers should be CEOs, COOs, CFOs, Support Function Leaders, General Managers and Managers throughout a firm.

Price--$29.95

CAPACITY MEASUREMENT & IMROVEMENT

Authors: CAM-I Capacity Model Interest Group

In a competitive economy, the effective use of capacity is critical. Unfortunately, there has been no universal approach to measuring the effectiveness of capacity use. The model explained in this book provides this missing tool. The model helps evaluate and change how companies use and plan capacity.

Capacity Measurement & Improvement shows how capacity measurement can be used to provide strategic information that can help managers improve the productivity of existing capacity and facilitate intelligent capital investment decisions.

The concepts of the capacity model came from work by H. L. Gantt, published in 1916, where he focused on identifying causes of variability and waste along with organizational responsibilities for capacity. This book puts these ideas into the current organizational environment.

"Capacity Measurement & Improvement" presents; 1) A unique capacity model, researched and developed by CAM-I; 2) Templates for application and implementation procedures; 3) Straightforward definitions; and 4) Key point summaries and illustrations to facilitate reader understanding

Price--$34.95

SERVICE PROCESS MEASUREMENT: BREAKING THE CODE

Authors: K. Euske, Norm Frause, T. Peck, Bruce Rosenstiel, Steve Schreck

This document provides a comprehensive and systematic approach to developing and applying activity-based performance measurements to processes that provide services - i.e., activities that usually have tangible outputs - within organizations. While there is extensive literature on analyzing operational processes within manufacturing organizations, there is little analysis available of service processes in either manufacturing or service organizations. This guidebook is intended to remedy that gap and to help seasoned process managers further enhance their organization's efficiency by extending the application of activity-based management and performance measurements to service processes.

This document is organized to lead the reader from the identification and analysis of the service process to the development of performance measures and an understanding of cost relationships, and includes case studies that illustrate using this approach for enhancing the performance of an organization's service processes.

Price--$19.95

THE CLOSED LOOP: IMPLEMENTING ACTIVITY-BASED PLANNING & BUDGETING

Editors: Stephen C. Hansen & Robert G. Torok

The CAM-I Activity-Based Planning and Budgeting Interest Group consists of managers of budgeting processes, consultants to enterprises developing and using budgets, planning and budgeting software developers and academics. All were dismayed by the abysmal state of budgeting as they keenly felt many of the problems with current practice. This book contains their thoughts and new approach.

Although current budgeting practices and processes have many problems, the budget is here to stay.

The Closed-Loop Model reflects a powerful new budgeting approach that speaks to many of the problems associated with traditional budgets and budgeting processes while retaining and enhancing the benefits obtained from the process.

Specifically, the Closed-Loop Model and ABPB Process:

- Reduces the need for extrapolating prior year's numbers,
- Reduces the time to perform each budget interaction,
- Explicitly analyzes and incorporates capacity,
- Removes the shroud of secrecy over budget deliberations,
- Increases employee buy-in, and
- Can reduce gaming.

Price--$29.95

ACTIVITY-BASED COST MANAGEMENT DESIGN FRAMEWORK: "Getting It Right The First Time"

Editors: Ronald R. Bleeker & Kenneth J. Euske

The mission of CAM-I's ABCM Design Framework is to assist first-time implementers and experienced practitioners alike with having successful Activity-Based Cost Management system deployments. It includes the comprehensive and disciplined approaches that have been "tested in the trenches" and fully validated.

The work is the culmination of four long years of cross-industry collaboration reviewing lessons learned, reasons for failure and requirements for success. The project contributors represented some 140[+] years of collective ABCM implementation experience….arguably the most seasoned research team ever assembled in the CAM-I consortium's 32 year history. To that end the Design Framework should be considered a mandatory reference for any practitioner charged with the responsibility of implementing and maintaining an Activity-Based Costing system.

A companion web-enabled and user-friendly toolset is also available to CAM-I members to make compilation of the assessment data painless and its analysis effortless. With this wealth of information, this robust tool further insures that organizations are best positioned to avoid the typical pitfalls for first-time implementers and achieve successful and sustainable systems for ongoing decision support.

Price--$29.95